THE UNGREEN PARK

GILL BRASON
The Ungreen Park
The Diary of a Keeper

THE BODLEY HEAD
LONDON SYDNEY
TORONTO

To two Brians
and
to Ronnie,
my new workmate

British Library Cataloguing
in Publication Data
Brason, Gill
The ungreen park
1. Islington (London Borough)—Social life and customs 2. Children in Islington (London Borough) 3. Islington (London Borough)—Parks 4. Islington (London Borough)—Playgrounds
I. Title
942.1'43 DA685.I8
ISBN 0-370-30088-2

© Gill Brason 1978
Printed in Great Britain for
The Bodley Head Ltd
9 Bow Street London WC2E 7AL
by Cox and Wyman Ltd, Fakenham
Set in Monotype Plantin Light
First published 1978

Introduction

I have been working as a park-keeper in the Islington area for the past two years, and I seem to have fallen in love with the place and the people. Other parts of London have their own fascination but never have I encountered such colourful contrasts as there are here.

If you were to visit Islington for the first time you could not fail to be intrigued. Get off the tube at Highbury Station and cross Upper Street and simply keep turning corners; you will find yourself walking from one world into another at almost every turn. One minute you are standing in a beautiful Georgian square: tall, elegant, white houses with rococo ceilings and marble fireplaces, inhabited by tall, elegant, self-assured people. Turn a corner and you find yourself in a narrow street reeking of decay: tenement houses built at the turn of the century for the artisan-shopkeeper class and now inhabited by poor families who have been on the rehousing list for years. Washing hangs over the crumbling balconies, cats prowl and children squall in a Hogarthian morass.

Turn another corner or walk through a park and you come to neat rows of three-storeyed terraced houses with brass door-knockers and the occasional carriage lamp. Neat little cars outside the doors, an air of benign complacency about the well-scrubbed steps, the crisp white curtains.

Keep on walking and you will come to the building site where they are putting up three-storeyed council flats for slum clearance 'victims'. Next door to the site is the little concrete park where I am working at present. When the flats are finished they are supposed to be going to do something about redeveloping the play area for the kids. I don't suppose we will get half the things we really need. Lack of funds is always a ready excuse. But if we could only have a play-house, a small football pitch, a few more swings, some patches of grass, and some sensitivity and thought about the replanning, what a difference it could make.

All of us who work in the parks staged a one-day strike recently in protest at the vast amount spent on flowers for the Mayor's do. How about the children who do not live in the elegant squares and cannot afford to go into the Sobell Centre? What about the lack of recreational facilities for the not so well-off? Well may the ratepayers complain about the local authority's sense of priorities!

The three parks I have worked on varied very strongly in character.

The first one was around Canonbury, and I encountered the Islington trendies with their plump children all in dungarees (why do the *nouveau riche* wear patched workmen's clothes?), their shockingly affected accents and boring pretentiousness. I also met the children from the ugly tenement buildings, who seemed far more real and ready to establish a relationship. Unfortunately, just when I was getting to know them I was moved to the Barbican.

I found that park, just off the City Road, a truly depressing place, with the great high-rise flats lowering down menacingly at the little people running and squabbling and playing beneath them. These skyscrapers actually seemed to have an expression on their faces, almost human. Disdainful stones suddenly prised up from the grey rockery gazing without pity at the teeming ants beneath them.

In the Barbican I met what the social workers call 'problem families' and some of my best and most loyal friends, like Tom and Martin, who followed me when I left to work on another even smaller patch of concrete, down the New North Road. That is where I encountered the National Front, the Sniffers, the Muggers and the Junkies and—not to be confused with these others—the delightful Debbie.

I do not profess to be an anthropologist or a sociologist. I simply wanted to portray honestly and without rancour, or too much analysis, the tragi-comedy played out before me. So I wrote down my experiences as they happened—sometimes the same evening when I got home, sometimes a few days later, but always as soon as I had the opportunity, so that their freshness should not be lost.

This book is a tribute to the children of Islington, a few of whom I have had the pleasure of getting to know during a very formative part of their lives. I have a tremendous affection for the people among whom I have worked, and I hope it shows. I admire their toughness, their guts, their sense of humour and their tremendous generosity. None of them has very much, but they all want to give.

They have so little here, down the New North Road. No flowers or water, not even a sand-pit. Yet even in these concrete surroundings the children are still developing into people—young trees growing in the ungreen park.

Brian's Park

That hounded feeling. Escape to Regent's Park and solitude. Away from the hustle and harassment of Oxford Street, the arrogance of Regent Street, the tin-bell tinkle of the yellow-robed bovver kids chanting 'Hari! Hari!', the elegant cool bars where women flutter and fantasise and men strut and sympathise—insincerely. I've had enough. On the spur of the moment I walk out of my good job, my successful career.

I know exactly where I am going. To see the best friend I have ever had, to find the broad shoulders I have so often cried on. When everything seemed too much there was always Brian and the comfort of a chess game, coffee, restful music. He knew how to sleep in the afternoon under the shade of the lime tree in the little Tufnell Park garden full of tin cans, cats and tangled mauve and yellow weeds.

I cross into Portland Place and pause for a moment to look up at the building where there is said to be a nest of kestrels. I do not see any birds today, but maybe they are sleeping or the parents are out foraging for scraps somewhere. How brave of the family to live high above the great red London buses snorting at the traffic lights like big sweating beasts of burden.

Entering the park makes me gasp with pleasure. Everywhere is so green and time has blissfully stood still. Tourists are strolling around sedately and there is an air of calm about everyone's movements. My pace slows, all my anger and aggression gone.

I sit on a bench and watch a young man with sun-bleached surf-rider's hair, naked to the waist, gently hosing the pink and red roses. He looks beautiful in his absorption, yet exquisitely indolent. Two hours ago I felt white-faced, desk bound, imprisoned in my own image. Now I am free. I have joined the ranks of the unemployed.

I envy the young man the simplicity of his work, his closeness to nature. I watch him pause, take out a handkerchief, mop his brow.

'Excuse me.'

He grins. 'Yes?'

'How did you get such a lovely job?'

'All yer got to do is apply to yer local council.'

His broad-vowelled cockney accent does not detract from his Adonis-like appearance. Men are beautiful when they are golden.

'Thanks, I will.' And I give him a frank smile of appraisal. Whatever is happening to me? I feel vaguely lustful and the way we are looking at one another is strange and almost frightening. I stand up, very conscious of his eyes upon me.

'What's the hurry?'

'I have to meet someone.'

'Lucky fellow.'

'How do you know it's a fellow?' I say archly, astonished at my own boldness.

He laughs. 'Have a nice day, love. Don't stay out in the sun too long.'

I cross the park, walking more briskly. Going to see Brian soon. I come to the elegant, expensive block of flats off St John's Wood High Street and stand beneath them anxiously scanning the tops of the tall imposing building where Brian is working as a restorer. At length I see a little ant-like figure in green overalls, precariously perched in a cradle about a hundred feet up in the air. I call his name but he is so high that he cannot hear me and then I see that there are half a dozen tiny figures in green dotted around the top storeys of these magnificent flats. How fragile the little men look. How frightening not even to know which of those minute beings is actually Brian.

It is best if I wait until they come down for their lunch break. I sit on a wall with my back to the mansions, no longer able to watch. Brian has described his job to me but I have never realised quite how dangerous the work really is. My problems pale into insignificance and the false world I have just rejected seems trivial and far away by comparison.

A squat, well-dressed woman carrying a chihuahua approaches me.

'Have you seen the agent?' She demands in a voice which invites subservience.

I blink stupidly: 'What agent?'

She glares at my new white trouser-suit. 'About the new apartment for sale.'

'I know nothing about it.'

She surveys me pugnaciously through her polaroids. 'Are you by any chance waiting for the agent?'

'No. I'm waiting for my bloke to come down off the scaffold.'

She looks incredulous and, lost for words, turns and stumps away aggressively.

Brian has come down from the cradle. We are sitting in the public bar of a little High Street pub eating cheese rolls and drinking lager. I keep wanting to reach out and touch him and make sure he is there and not a hundred feet up in the air.

'So there you have it. My marriage is up the spout. The bailiffs want their pound of flesh and so does the bank manager. My husband is off to Denmark to study the theatre, and God knows where he got the money from, and now I'm out of work.'

He calmly sips his beer. 'Any more problems, luv?' he says in his quiet Yorkshire accent.

I have to laugh. There is about him a resilience, a toughness I have never suspected before. He gives a slow freckled grin. 'So you're free this afternoon?'

'Of course I'm free,' I snorted. 'Never been so bloody free in me life.'

He sits placidly nibbling at his roll. 'I won't bother going back to the scaffold. Fancy taking a boat out this afternoon? We can just drift and talk. It's quiet on the canal.'

'Great.'

'I often do that. Sometimes I just lie in the boat reading, and birds and ducks come up and look at me.'

As we talked that afternoon it became clear to us both that we should move in together. He reassured me that it did not matter what I did, he would take care of me until I found my feet again. As for jobs, why not go ahead and do what I liked for a change? Follow my inclinations; I had no need to be the breadwinner any more. What did I really want to do?

Write, but there never seemed to be any time.

'In that case, find something which inspires you to write and which involves you in a way you want to be involved.'

Maybe it was symbolic that we had tied the boat up under a tree. We weren't drifting with the current any more.

'You have to make things happen,' he said simply.

Ever since that afternoon's long, slow, lazy row and relaxed, comforting conversation I have associated Regent's Park with Brian. In fact now I always refer to it as 'Brian's Park'. . .

I began to make things happen. Together we went flat-hunting. It was a soul-destroying business. When my divorce came through we would be able to move back into my own flat; meanwhile Brian and I could really only afford one room.

In Camden Town the bed-sitters were bleak and grimy. All over Holloway fierce landladies with dressmakers' dummies in their windows stared pointedly at my abdomen. I wore no wedding ring—why live a lie?—and no doubt they wanted to assure themselves that their potential source of income would be trouble-free. Not being pregnant, I presumably passed muster, but it is amazing how offensive such an inspection can be made by an expert, and nothing would have induced me to live at close quarters with these women. Hackney seemed full of slippery stairs with the banisters painted the inevitable shit-brown colour, and frying smells.

It all seemed so hopeless and sordid and seamy at first. If we had been ten years younger we might have found the situation romantic, but we had both been around too much and our search for cheap accommodation seemed a regressive step. But what was the alternative?

Eventually, I managed to find us a room in Muswell Hill. The landlord wanted a month's deposit and thirteen pounds a week rent but at least it was clean and private and only for six months. It seemed strange to be living in such a confined space after having had my own flat for eight years. There were many minor irritations: having to wait ages to use the bathroom and then finding a dark black ring around the tub; making sure we had enough change for the meter; being woken up in the middle of the night by David Bowie records being played loudly overhead. One can take such discomforts in one's stride at eighteen but we both found them a bit enervating at thirty.

There were compensations. There was a big communal back garden where we could sit and play chess. There were lilac trees and fir trees, and squirrels which we fed; they would approach us with great boldness and seemed surprisingly tame. At night when you sat on the little john under the eaves you could hear owls hooting. There were long walks in Highgate Woods. The young people in the house did not bother us and we did not bother them. We never complained about the nocturnal music. Let them enjoy their freedom.

Meanwhile our relationship, which had been practically platonic for eight years, ripened and matured into something much stronger and more tangible. It all started that day in 'Brian's Park'.

Joining the Parks

'There's no need for you to get a job if you don't want to, luv. Get your notebooks out and a typewriter and go and sit under that tree in the garden.'

Brian's offer sounded tempting, but my nature is very independent and the prospect of somebody actually keeping me was not one that I relished.

However, I was glad not to have to worry too much about the status of the jobs I took on. I wanted to get amongst ordinary people who did not talk in riddles and did not have cash-register eyes and knives ready to stab you in the back while they called you 'darling'. I wanted to be with people who had no pretensions, no front, and who said what they meant and meant what they said. A lot of Brian's Yorkshire bluntness was rubbing off on me. Consequently, I had tremendous fun rediscovering my own identity. Nobody was my keeper.

It was most stimulating to be away from the employment agency where I had worked for the past eight years. Walking out of that sleek, sophisticated world into Regent's Park had been one of the best things I had ever done. 'You must change your life' is the last line of a poem by Rilke; I had decided to change mine, drastically.

I applied for a job on the council parks, and was immediately given an interview. The man I saw was small and suntanned, with timid brown eyes, and I took an immediate liking to him. He was very kind and optimistic. He asked me if I liked children and I said I did, although at that time I knew little about them and hardly ever came into contact with them—the question rather worried me. He took down a few scanty details; I was surprised that he did not seem to want to know more about my background. It was most refreshing to be taken at face value, and his casual, jovial approach helped to restore my faith in human nature. One thing I didn't tell him was that I had 'O' and 'A' levels. I was afraid that if I mentioned them I would get stuck in some fusty-smelling office round the back of the Town Hall. I wanted to be a real person, simply one of the people, to be able to observe and to contemplate objectively, which is impossible if you are given a fancy title and too much status. He more or less promised me a job later on—they wouldn't be taking on any new park-keepers until the spring, he said, but he asked me to come back then. I promised that I would.

For the next few months I did any and every job that came my way. I distributed papers in the street, helped out in the markets, charred, typed accounts, tried to find jobs for the junkies, and sold advertising space. These were all interesting and useful experiences, which widened my horizons. Best of all, I started writing articles and getting them accepted and I found I was writing poetry again, something I thought I could not do any more.

When I returned to the council office in April, the same pleasant man greeted me enthusiastically.

'Can you start on Monday?' he asked without hesitation.

'Of course.'

'Good. Well, here are the keys to your park. It's in Canonbury.' (He drew me a little map and gave me a time-sheet.) 'Report there at three o'clock and the person you are to work with will show you the ropes.'

'Great.' I walked out into Holloway Road feeling exhilarated and excited. I was looking forward to giving Brian the news.

The little park where I was to start work looked exceptionally pretty that April afternoon. There were three small parks very close together and although the surface of the playground part was concrete this did not strike me as ugly because surrounding it were pink may trees which were just in flower and small ponds where I could see ducks and fluffy ducklings.

I let myself in with the key the council had given me and stood under the trees looking over at the little hut. It was tiny, painted yellow, with a pointed roof and a decorative ball on the top. I was enchanted with my Wendy-house. In fact, I was completely captivated by the entire scene. Looking round I could see a climbing frame, two sets of swings, the ones with bars across obviously intended for the under-fives, an 'umbrella' roundabout, a smaller one shaped like a top, a see-saw, a kind of rocking-horse affair with seats inside, a slide and a big sand-pit. There was something missing. I furrowed my brows and tried to concentrate. Ah yes, I remembered from my own childhood. Boat-swings. They had always been my favourites. I had always been the daring one who did the 'working up', bending my body at decidedly hazardous angles as we went higher and higher, dreading the unexpected arrival of my mother who had expressly forbidden this pastime until I was bigger and wiser.

It struck me as strange that there was no one there to meet me, but I assumed they had been held up, and sat quite contentedly munching sausage sandwiches, the pink blossom falling in a soft fine dust around me.

The park was empty, because it was only three o'clock and the children were still in school. I suppose I would have been quite happy to have gone on simply sitting in that nostalgic little garden but after about an hour a steady April shower started. There was nowhere for me to shelter and I was only wearing a light jacket over my jeans. I could not get into the hut until the other keeper arrived.

A plump-faced man in a beret walked towards me, carrying a spade. He looked like an onion-seller but in fact turned out to be a gardener.

'Excuse me,' I called.

He came swaggering over in his old corduroys and Wellingtons.

'You lost?' he asked accusingly as though I were to blame.

'I'm waiting for someone and they haven't turned up.'

Head on one side, he studied me as though I were a candidate for Friern Barnet lunatic asylum.

'So what! That's life. Won't I do instead?'

He grinned wolfishly, exposing the most horrible teeth.

'No. You don't understand. I'm supposed to start work here. Today. I can't get into the hut and,' I added crossly, 'I'm rather wet.'

He scratched his head slowly, still regarding me as though I were the local lunatic.

'Well there wouldn't be anyone 'ere,' he said calmly. 'Stands to reason.'

I was beginning to get really annoyed with the man and his deliberate vagueness. He had the insolence of 'Mellors' and he was enjoying my situation greatly.

'Why is that?'

He pushed a finger up one nostril and began to jiggle it around meditatively. I looked away.

'They're all in the Town 'all,' he answered at length.

'What are they doing in there?' I was beginning to feel more and more like Alice in Wonderland.

The man took his spade away from his shoulder, stood it in front of him and leaned on it.

'Union meeting.' He spat contemptuously, mercifully over my right shoulder. 'That's what I think of unions.'

'Should I go up there, then?'

'You'd better, unless . . .' He leaned closer so that I could see the small hairs sprouting from his nose, '. . . you want to come in my little 'ut and dry off.'

'No thanks.' I stood up hurriedly. I felt like adding: 'Don't feel like any forget-me-not fancies, thank you,' but imagined any literary allusions would be lost on him.

As I was walking up to the Town Hall the shower suddenly stopped and I looked up and saw the beginnings of a rainbow which I hoped would be a good omen. I had never been into the Town Hall before, except once to report a missing dustbin, and I felt slightly intimidated by the archaic grandeur of the imposing building.

The commissionaire was elderly, very helpful, but on the deaf side.

'Excuse me.' I smiled at him. 'I started on the parks today and I can't get into the hut on my park.'

'You can't find anywhere to park your car, madam?'

'No.' I was on the verge of giggles. 'Isn't there a meeting on today?'

'This way, madam.' And he started to lead me up a splendid flight of stairs with ornate banisters on either side of them. At the top, he knocked timidly on a door and a haughty secretary wearing pink-framed spectacles came out.

'Yes?' she asked impatiently.

'This lady had trouble parking her car and has come to the meeting.'

'The meeting of the Town Council?' She eyed me with some surprise. (I suppose you do get the odd councillor arriving at a meeting wearing denims, but not with tangled wet hair, looking like a bedraggled Yorkshire terrier.)

'Look,' I explained patiently to them both, feeling damp and miserable, 'I think I'm in the wrong place. I said nothing about a car. I haven't even got a car. I started work on the park today.'

The woman peered at me short-sightedly and I prayed that her hearing was better than her eyesight.

'On the parks!' she exclaimed incredulously, in a voice which Dame Edith would have been proud of.

'That's right,' I muttered uncomfortably.

'Well, what on earth are you doing up here?'

'I really don't know. Although I was supposed to start work I couldn't get into the hut on my park. I was told they were all up at the Town Hall so I came along to the meeting.'

A frown of distaste furrowed her perfect brows and she

looked as though there was a bad smell under her nose. I felt like farting with disgust.

'Oh, you mean the Union meeting? Downstairs. In the basement.' And she shut the door in our faces. I could have spat.

As the poor commissionaire led me down the long steep staircase into the bowels of the building I commiserated with him about class-distinction and silly jumped-up secretaries. He kept nodding his head and I think he understood the general drift of what I was saying for as he deposited me outside the right place he winked and patted my shoulder.

I entered a vast room which seemed to be full of men wearing donkey-jackets and Wellington boots and all shouting at the tops of their voices. Everyone seemed to be using four-letter words very freely. I did not understand what was going on; so many people were talking at once. It was something to do with rates of pay, someone had been driving another man's tractor when he should not have been, and were they going to unite with the dustmen and strike next Wednesday? What on earth had I got myself into?

A little woman with high-piled blonde hair approached me and apologised for not being at the park to meet me.

When the meeting finally ended she led me back to the gardens of Canonbury and handed over the hut keys.

I asked about the lavatory.

'There ain't one 'ere, love. You should 'ave gone in the Town 'all. Only the Gents is open.' And she went and stood protectively outside while I walked into the foul-smelling urinal.

What a start!

For a short time I was very happy in Canonbury. I got to know the gardeners; even the awesome 'Mellors' turned out to be a decent enough bloke in his own way, although I steered well clear of his hut.

I took excursions down New River Walk, a small but

rambling park with rockeries and shrubberies and little pools containing goldfish. John was Polish and very proud of his garden. He showed me round, telling me the long Latin names for his plants, and I wish I could remember them all but find it impossible. John sometimes used to cry in sheer frustration when the kids came in and tore up the delicate flowers and bulbs he had just planted and I would commiserate with him at such pointless vandalism.

Irish Joe who looked after the park with the pink mayblossom was very considerate to me in those early days. He helped me to sweep up at night, chased the big boys with a broom and showed me the ducks' nests. He was quiet and gentle and we would sometimes go for a Guinness together after work when he would tell me how proud he was of his children; one was a teacher and the other a civil servant.

One morning, he tapped on my hut door and said excitedly: 'There's something you must see.'

Outside in the busy main street all the traffic had come to a standstill. Big lorries stood snorting at the zebra crossing. The mother duck and her brood of ducklings were waddling across the road. They were half-way over when she stopped abruptly and went back to check that her entire family was following her. 'She's counting them,' whispered Joe. Reassured that all eight children were present and correct, and disdainfully ignoring the rush-hour, she slowly went on her way. I wished I had a camera.

Jackie

Sometimes the park is very peaceful and there are no children, so that I can sit in my hut and catch up with my reading. At other times there are so many children in the playground that I am frightened to leave them for one moment, even to go to the lavatory.

It worries me sometimes being responsible for up to forty little kids. I am not afraid of responsibility as such but my experience of it has always been with adults. Yet what are children if not small adults?

Over the past three weeks I have noticed that there are certain personalities which predominate. The more extrovert characters tend to congregate around my hut. It is with these children that I have the most adult conversations.

Jackie is fourteen and looks a good eighteen. Her platform shoes have elevated her to five-foot six. She has rather pretty, long, naturally blonde hair and blue eyes, and is worried about the spots that keep appearing around her chin. She seems to be a very domesticated girl, always helping me to sweep up the sand-pit and the pink blossom from the grounds.

She is protective in the extreme towards the younger children. A kind of substitute mother. She was telling me about a little girl of six who had been brutally sexually assaulted in the flats.

'That was a year ago and they're still looking for the man what done it. He was quite an ordinary, decent-looking youngish bloke in a suit. Her insides will never be the same again. She's had three operations and she's only seven. They don't think she'll ever be able to have a baby.'

I told Jackie that I was constantly on the look-out for

'funny men' in the park. This particular kind of pervert is to my mind the most tragic and the most difficult to understand.

My only fear is that I might make a mistake. There must be perfectly innocent lonely sorts of people who derive pleasure from children's company. There is one such man—he looks Turkish or Cypriot and hardly speaks any English. He is constantly sitting in the playground and standing by the swings, always smiling at the children. I have watched him very carefully and can detect nothing out of order about his behaviour. I would not dream of tackling him, but I never leave the park while he is around. Just in case.

Doris

Doris said: 'I'd rather go to bed and read a good book.' She had come down to see me in the park. Her legs were stockingless and speckled with blue veins. She wore a flowered scarf over her dandelion-coloured hair. I sat in the hut beside her with my flask between us. It was raining outside so I could not go out into the children's playground.

'When you get to my age you don't want to be bothered with all that.'

'How old are you, Doris?'

'Forty-three. My mother had a bad time of it when she was forty-five. Early change, see. It's all this physical work, see. Makes you tired at night. Getting up at five and clean-out those offices. No energy at night. My old man's a selfish old bugger. Expects too much of me. It's all right for him. He works on the buildings. All men that work on the buildings get randy at night. Something to do with the open-air life. I can understand why. Working with those electric drills does it. All the vibration. Now if I hadn't four kids I might think different. I started carrying when I was seventeen. That's far too young. I was only a baby myself.'

Doris lives in the council flats opposite my little park. I cannot make tea in the hut because there is something wrong with the water. I bring my flask to work and Doris comes over at five for a cup of tea.

'Now when I was your age I couldn't get enough of it and he didn't want to know. We even got a package tour to Spain one summer because I thought the hot climate might turn him on. I tried everything, but it wouldn't rise up. Now it's the other way round.

'This woman who had the playground before you was a dirty cow. She used to have a man in the hut. A gardener from one of the other parks. We could see everything from our bedroom window.'

I knew this could not possibly be true as Doris slept in her front room, which overlooked Upper Street.

'Men will never understand us women. Now I like a rude book. I like them letters in *Forum*. I like reading about it. The things that some people get up to. You would have to be a contortionist. You ever tried anything like that?'

'A couple of times.'

'Oh Gill, what a girl you are! On the pill are you?'

'Yes.'

'Don't you ever want kids now, then?'

'I've almost got past the stage. It's just so bloody impractical.'

'Can't say I blame you, girl. Eleven pounds a week to live in a bleedin' council flat. Rates just gone up again. Ten pence on a packet of fags. Two pence on a pint of beer. How the hell are we supposed to keep kids when we can't even keep ourselves?'

'I don't know, Doris.'

'Everyone crammed into rabbit warrens. No privacy.

Walls so thin that you can hear everyone having it off regular as clockwork Sunday afternoon just after "Double Your Money".'

'Homosexuality is very much on the increase.'
'Funny you should say that. Stands to reason, don't it? When there's no chance of family life what's the point of going with someone of the opposite sex? People most probably turn queer because of bad accommodation. One of the girls at work has this right old bat of a landlady. She can't bring her fellow back for a cup of tea but she can have her girl-friends in till all hours. The young bloke lives in one of them common lodging-houses. You know the kind I mean. Two or three men in one room. It's encouraging them to turn bent.'

'There was an article I read somewhere. They put a whole load of rats in a very small space and studied their reactions. Well, the female rats stopped breeding and there was a lot of fighting and scrapping. Eventually, the males started pairing up together and the females did the same. The only rats that survived were the ones who crept to the top of the cage. The plutocrats. They sat apart eating and looking down in contempt on the rabble below. They grew sleek and fat. It's an interesting analogy with present-day life in London.'

Doris scratches her head in perplexity.

'Wish you wouldn't use such long words, love. All this education.'

'I educated myself, Doris. I can't stop reading.'
'Like this job in the park, do you?'
'Well at least I can sit here reading when it rains.'
'Terrible kids you have to look after. Blame their parents.'
'I like the kids, Doris.'
'They're a rough lot. Beats me how you can put up with them. All that glass in the sand-pit. All the violence.'

The rain has stopped and the flask is empty. I unlock the

hut and walk out into the playground to untie the swings. Doris walks with me in her pink fluffy fat slippers, skilfully avoiding the puddles.

Soon the playground begins to fill with my adoptive children. I draw a deep breath. There is a beautiful smell—almost a taste—of green grass and wet earth. The daffodils quiver in sympathy.

I turn my back on the council flats, pick sticky little Deidre up and lift her into the swing.

Colin, Pat, Guy

I've only been working for the council for three weeks and already they've decided to move me. I am not altogether surprised—I have broken nearly every rule in the book. However, the culminating factor was probably my getting up a petition for a new football pitch and a play-house for the kids around Canonbury.

There has been no violence or vandalism in my playground since I took over. In my attempt to reach the sullen thirteen- to fifteen-year-olds who sat aggressively smoking on the children's swings I tried to give them a sense of identification and belonging. They seemed to accept me; some of them even confided in me. The way I dressed was not unlike their own casual modern style, and they didn't think of me as someone from a different background.

My own adolescence had been a time of great rebellion. At fourteen I wore tight yellow jeans and fluorescent socks, and nicked my father's razor-blades, sewing them inside my belt. I fancied myself as a teddy-boy's moll. So I could hardly condemn the same tendencies in these kids.

We talked about many things. Violence. Frustration.

Aggression. What led up to it. Together, we discussed self-motivation as opposed to moronic conformity. Colin talked to me more than any of the others. He was rather good-looking with yellow, fashionably long hair. Invariably, whatever the weather, he wore a trendy tweed sports coat which flapped elegantly around the calves of his checked trousers. He felt inadequate and underprivileged. At nearly sixteen he had a passive acceptance of life. What could possibly lie ahead of him but the factory floor, some menial apprenticeship scheme, the inevitable young marriage, the council flat, Friday nights out with the boys while the wife goes to Bingo? He visualised clearly the gaudy trappings of status symbols, colour-TV sets, hi-fi equipment, a new bike for the eldest child.

Where was he going? He was intelligent enough to know. The half-child, half-man in him rebelled. He was at a cross-roads in his life and was utterly confused and quite terrified at the prospect of leaving school. He tried desperately to cling to some vestige of his childhood but he still had to assert his manhood.

Colin smoked and swore and described his sexual experiences with a worldly cynicism. Yet he sat, pathetically large, in the children's swing. He felt utterly alone, and could not come to terms with being in the lowest stream of the comprehensive school. He did not seem to play any games or even enjoy records. Although he spoke contemptuously about girls he had 'had', and said so-and-so was a 'slag', he was probably, to all intents and purposes, mentally and physically a virgin.

I hardly ever saw him laugh until one Saturday. Guy was holding an unlit match under a magnifying-glass, concentrating the sun's heat on to it. At the first sign of smoke, Colin burst out laughing in ecstasy: 'Let's burn the fucking playground down!'

I am no psychologist, but I cannot help realising that this desire to smash up objects, particularly symbols of childhood, is occasioned by the tragedy of never have really been a child. You treat something you have never really enjoyed with utter contempt, and if you have had a slight taste of the pleasure but never experienced it to the full, the contempt is all the greater.

Pat walks in wearing her stilts. She is a big-built blonde girl and finds it difficult to get away with half-fare on the bus. She goes to a school which sounds progressive and intelligent in approach. Pat has a job in a shop on Saturdays and during the school holidays. She had to get a special permit as she is only fourteen. At her school the children are allowed to specialise in the subjects they like. Pat has a head for figures and finds working as a cashier in a cake shop a good preparation for adult life. A thoroughly sensible girl with no grievances. If I had a daughter like Pat I would not be worried.

Of course she is on the 'pill', but this is mainly to stop painful periods. She is the archetype of the girl next door. Sane, wholesome and ordinary. She will obviously make someone a good wife and mother one day.

Guy is fourteen and passionately interested in prehistoric animals. He has just brought an evil-looking model of a dinosaur for my inspection. The monster stands about a foot high and is painted emerald green and appears to be double-jointed. Guy is making a kind of miniature horror-film involving neolithic men being devoured by these creatures. Everyone admires 'Fred' and even Colin shows a world-weary interest in the proceedings.

Guy and I had a conversation about the petition for the play-house. Everyone became very enthusiastic. We could show monster-films, play records, put on a Punch and Judy show for the little ones, etc.

'How many signatures you got now, keep?' asks Guy.

'About four hundred.'

'Terrific. Fucking marvellous!'

At least while they are enthusiastic about the petition

they are not smashing things up. But I reckoned without the attitude of the council, and I was moved.

On almost my last morning in Canonbury I wandered into Joe's park and watched the pink blossom lying like soft blanket-down on the river. The drake with his green satin head bobbed over to his mate. She sat brown and bedraggled, a little mousy female who would never be able to assert herself by wearing brighter, rebellious plumage. What freedom we humans have by comparison!

Nola

So I have been sent into exile in disgrace. I am now in the wilds of the Barbican. Everything strikes me as grey. The great high-rise flats, the concrete park, even the pigeons look dull and nondescript. I merge with the landscape, camouflaged in my dark old cords and grey schoolboy's V-neck from the Oxfam shop.

Tentatively, I approach the hut where I am to relieve the other keeper. I have come on duty early as a special favour because I want to start out right. When you do shift work with another person it is very important to maintain a good relationship. This means relieving them half an hour early so they can get away, covering for them when they are sitting in the pub if the foreman calls, filling the kettle at night and stocking up the tea-caddy before it gets too low. All little, simple things, but showing a friendly sensitivity which is always appreciated.

I did not know what this woman was going to be like and I knocked gently on the hut door. There was no reply. I peered in. In a cosy little room she sat ensconced in a big old armchair, head thrown back, mouth slightly open, a little dark plump woman in her fifties, snoring loudly. I let myself in very quietly and put the kettle on, careful not to wake her. I like studying people when they are asleep and I came to the conclusion that she was the type I would hit it off with, rough-and-ready but kind.

A cup stood on the table beside her and I picked it up. To my amazement it contained a set of false teeth. I burst out laughing and the woman woke up.

'Jaysus!' she exclaimed in a thick Irish brogue.

I smiled 'Hello'. I liked her eyes. They were very brown and merry and slightly wicked. She stood up and stretched herself, scratched her back in the too-tight overall. 'Me name is Nola. What do they call you?'

'Gill.'

She immediately made me feel welcome, bustling around and mothering me, showing me how to make toast on the old electric fire, chattering all the time.

'This is a very cushy number. Most of the time I do be kipping.'

'Don't you get any children in here?'

'We do be at times but I chases them out. They don't like me at all. Calling me "old bag" they are, and "Nitty Nola" and worse. But I don't care. I'm strict and I shout at them. I don't like the black ones. They're very cheeky so I shouts at them and they calls back: "Up the IRA".' She laughs to herself.

'But don't you get bored with no company?'

'I goes to kip or I read'—she indicates a pile of magazines—'sex stuff mostly.'

'Where's me teeth? Jaysus! I'm always losing them. I could feel something digging in me bum the other day and I found I was sitting on them.'

I indicated the tea-cup. 'You've been doing very well without them for the last ten minutes.'

She gave me a sharp look and I wondered if I had gone too far, but her eyes lit up with laughter.

'Sure I'm going to like you. You got any Irish in you by any chance?'

'My grandmother.'

'I might have guessed. Now what would I be doing with me teeth in the best cup?'

She had this great capacity for making fun of herself. Later I discovered that Nola and her false teeth were a standing joke amongst the children. When they came to me for water they would enquire anxiously: 'Have Nola's teeth been in that cup?'

Although it was four o'clock and time for her to knock off duty she seemed in no hurry to go and insisted on making more tea and toast.

'Were you not happy on the other park?'

'They weren't exactly happy with me. I got a petition up and let the kids play football and sit in the hut. The other woman I worked with was all right but she always seemed to have a broom in her hand. She used to complain about the park being left in a state.'

'Now don't you be worrying about that. I pays the kids to sweep up and sure I don't want to be killing meself from over-work.'

'I'll do my share. Don't worry. But I'm not a fanatic about cleaning.'

'You have to watch out for the autocratic children. Poor mites. They be always bashing their heads against the fence and screaming. Terrible it is to see.'

What was she talking about? Scratching my head, puzzled, I said: 'Very spoilt, are they? Do they have nannies and come from well-off families?'

'No. The poor things. Not a bit of it. They have a special school which brings them in here, with special teachers for them.'

'Oh, you mean autistic children.'

She looked at me and her eyes laughed merrily. 'I'm a divil with me words but that's what I do be meaning. They come in a special bus. I always makes a cup of tea for the teachers. Wonderful girls they are.'

I knew I was going to enjoy working with her. She was such a character! A combination of kindness—*sympatico* is the right word but untranslatable—and toughness. She was always making me bacon sandwiches, or cheese and spring onion, depending on the weather. She always wanted me to feel welcome. When I turned up half an hour early so that she could get away to do her shopping she rarely took advantage of it. She preferred to feed me—'You're too thin, girl' —and chat.

The kids were terrified of her, and she had a reputation for being very strict. However, she was strict for good reasons. For example, no one under seven was allowed on the slide; as it was a very high one, the rule was eminently sensible.

She was very unconsciously funny in the way the Irish often are. Her sense of humour was risqué but never crude.

One day we were sitting in the hut and I had just been throwing crumbs to the birds.

'I'm glad I'm not a pigeon.'

'Why is that?' The remark amused me, as she was a plump little soul with bright beady eyes and in some ways she resembled one.

'I'd hate to be a pigeon.'

'It's not a bad life if you get fed.'

Dramatically, she pointed out of the window at two birds in the act of copulation. 'When they have sex it's over in two seconds.'

Martin, Alf

From the recreation ground I can see blocks of high-rise flats and a bright yellow crane like a gigantic child's toy.

Martin is thin, wiry with glasses, and very small for fourteen. He possesses such a strong imagination that I sometimes wonder whether he can distinguish fact from fantasy. Today he wears blue jeans, a T-shirt printed with the words 'Super Specs', plimsolls with frayed red laces.

'I'm dead scared of Moorgate Station. Won't go down there on me own. I'm psychic, see, like me mum. That train-driver, him what crashed the tube, saw somefing.' Playing with his shoe-laces. 'Somefing out of the past. When they found him in the cab he was stood up with eyes staring like golf-balls. In the war there was all these people buried alive in the station. Stands to reason that he saw somefing. All those poor condemned souls down there. Every time a tube thunders by they relive the bombs. They ought to close it down. Don't you ever get scared round here, Gill? Know what this place used to be? An old burial ground for plague victims.'

I did not tell Martin that occasionally when the playground was deserted I could hear a sound like a thousand people sobbing and gibbering hopelessly. It was a very faraway sound. I have asked other people if they can hear this noise but so far no one admits that they can. I imagine that it is the wind whistling round the high-rise flats.

This morning my tame pigeon was waiting for me, squatting obsequiously outside the hut. He raised one seedy, yellow eye as I approached. If I do not appear immediately with a loaf of bread he raps imperiously on my battered green door with his beak.

Alf, as I have christened him, looks more individual than the other pigeons. They are a sort of slate-grey utilitarian colour. Alf is black, rakish and rather bedraggled. He looks as if he has been around.

After breakfast, and skilfully warding off the other pigeons who tend to peck at him with contempt, Alf goes and sits on the 'umbrella' roundabout. He gives me a sidelong glance out of his dissipated amber eye. At first, I pushed him around on the machine as a kind of joke, surprised that he stayed on it. Now his morning ride has become something of a ritual.

It is amusing to imagine someone out of my past walking into the park and watching me, Gillian Brason, aged thirty-three, former agency executive, pushing a pigeon round on a roundabout!

My only visitor this morning was a little white-haired enuretic woman who comes and sits on a bench titivating herself with mirror and lipstick. Today she asked me the same eternal question: 'Is my face clean?'

'Immaculate,' I assured her.

'Oh, I'm so glad. I'm going to meet my gentleman friend. What time do the pubs open?'

'Eleven o'clock.'

'And my coat isn't too long?'

It is a long, white, woollen, once-expensive coat which her gentleman friend bought her in a jumble sale.

'Just the right length.'

'I'm so glad.'

She shambles slowly away leaving an aroma of lavender water and urine behind her.

Today is Thursday, so I go along to the Town Hall to collect my wages. Everyone looks slightly ragged and shabby and sunburnt. I stand, one of only five women amongst a hundred men. Hands keep intruding themselves around various parts of my anatomy. I apply as much skill as I can muster to repelling the gropers. Then my name is called out and there is a bit of gay banter. 'Spend some on me, darlin'.'

Everyone looks amazingly fit, even the old stooped, gnarled men. Park-keepers or 'park people' seem to be a breed apart from other people. You have to be a bit of a loner. What normal person would like to sit on their own for up to thirteen hours a day?

I have my little hut where I can sit and boil myself an egg and make my tea. There is something very beautiful about the taste of eggs in the open air. I eat about six a day; great farmhouse eggs with yolks that seem to go on for ever. I feel as if I have never truly appreciated the taste of an egg before.

I cannot remember enjoying tastes or smells so vividly since I was a child. When I walk past a patch of grass which has been recently cut I feel I am literally drinking in the flavour of sweet grass as though it were some kind of nectar. I bit into a green apple this morning, and I enjoyed both the sharp flavour and the sound of my teeth rasping on the crisp skin.

The open-air life makes you feel perpetually randy, your skin tingles with the caress of the sun's rays and you are filled with an indolence that is quite blissful. What other way of life is there?

I've taken to reading poetry:

> *For skies of couple-colour as a brinded cow . . .*
> *Fresh fire coal chestnut-falls; finches' wings . . .*

Mavis

Mavis is my mate. She lives in a big concrete block of flats in the Barbican. On the eighteenth floor, so I don't go and see her very often as I don't like the lift. I make excuses and feel ashamed about not visiting her more frequently. She has to live in that building, poor bitch! Not me! I am not the social worker, who doesn't seem to be doing any good even though she has a degree. What does she know about life?

Mavis seems dissatisfied with the young woman looking after her case. 'She is the sort of girl I just can't talk to about sex with Alfie or nothink like that.' I met her once. About twenty-eight, tall, slim, immaculately groomed, but cold. She had a B.Sc., a Home Counties accent, and an 1100; and she didn't seem real. Had she ever really suffered? What could she know about the high-rise flats and how it felt to live in them, about bringing up four kids on twenty pounds a week? And how could she talk to you when your problem, as in Mavis's case, was definitely of a sexual nature? As Mavis put it: 'She's either a virgin, or a les, or both.'

Mavis, at twenty-four, looks thirty-four, worn out through childbearing, a sterilisation op., and a husband who beats her up whenever he is in a bad mood. In spite of all this, Mavis keeps up a jolly, resilient front. She is a very fat girl with glasses and straight, mousy hair. She is certainly no oil painting, but she can laugh at herself, and when she does she looks vivacious and her eyes crinkle prettily. I could not help liking her immensely from the first time I met her. In her own way she is a very brave girl. She is intelligent enough to realise that it is not too late to make something of herself.

Sometimes, when she was feeling very depressed and the kids were at school she would come over to the park. We would spend hours playing Monopoly, laughing and joking about being the last of the big spenders. I understand that the game was invented during the Depression in the thirties. The bloke who dreamed it up must have been a humanitarian. No wonder Monopoly is so popular in prison. In any event, it preoccupied us for four to six hours a day, and while we played she talked, and it was a relaxed way of talking. I never grew bored listening to Mavis.

Some people can unload all their problems on to you and you feel trapped, especially when they are just petty, nagging little worries common to us all. Not so with Mavis. Her descriptions of people and situations are colourful, almost Dickensian. She does not make me feel like a dustbin, as some people do, chucking all their emotional refuse into me. I squirm when they go into detailed descriptions of their operations and the state of their bowels. I am not squeamish, just bored out of my mind.

Mavis is a raconteur of the highest order. She made me feel as though I was living on the eighteenth floor, standing in the queue waiting for family income supplements, getting my purse nicked at the supermarket.

'Alfie gives me sixteen quid to do on for the week. I didn't have the nerve to tell him.' She paused, about to throw a dice.

'Do you want me to lend you a fiver?'

She frowned and pushed her glasses higher up her nose. 'Naw,' she said. 'I'd only have to give it you back. I'll fink of somethink.' Then, trying hard to dissipate the gloom which had fallen on us: 'Hey! You want a laugh? Guess what I caught Deidre doing?' Deidre is six. 'She got hold of Rupert's winkle in the bath.' Rupert is five. 'I told her to stop playing with him, of course. She says: "I wasn't playing with it, mum. Honest. I was just twisting it round."'

We both laughed uproariously. I threw the dice and moved my shoe to Liverpool Street. Feeling benevolent, I decided not to buy it as I knew she was collecting the stations.

A very strong friendship is beginning to form between myself and this big, tough, warm-hearted girl.

'There was something I wanted to ask you.' She paused, putting down the red and blue dice and lighting a Kensitas. 'Robert hasn't been christened yet. I was just wondering...' She halted, suddenly looking very shy, '... if you would be a godmother?'

I was startled, very flattered that she should think me worthy of such a position but at the same time somewhat panic-stricken.

'But I don't go to church or anything. I mean, would the vicar find me acceptable, and what would I have to do exactly?'

Robert was not a normal child. He was a very slow developer. Mavis had had twins, and the other child, a mongol, had died at two and a half. Now, at four, Robert could only speak in monosyllables but was tremendously loving and always coming to me for a cuddle. He had rather beautiful violet-coloured eyes and the only sign of mongol features was around his mouth. His favourite game with me was to come up and bash me gently on the head. Because of my shaggy yellow fringe he tended to think of me as a dog. When he hit me I would cover my face with both hands and pretend to cry. He would try to pull my hands away and give me a very wet kiss on the chin, saying: 'Ah! Poor dog!'

However, in the three months since I had known him I was pleased to notice definite progress. He was really learning to relate to objects and people. He knew which key from my bunch opened the door of my hut and he could put it into the lock, but he did not have the strength to turn it. He was destined for a special school, though I could not help feeling that he would have been better off with normal children.

The autistic and retarded children who came to play in the park nearly all had very vague eyes which rarely focused on you. Some walked in a disjointed, uncoordinated manner like clumsy marionettes. Some made strange, animal-like cries or groans as though they were in pain. They thought nothing of urinating in public or taking down their trousers in full view of the passing traffic. I could not really question the judgement of the qualified staff who had assigned Robert so early to one of these schools, but I did wonder with some trepidation how he would get on. Would they not hold back his development, I wondered?

And here was Mavis asking me to take on some of the responsibility. Was I adequate? Could I really cope?

'It's not that bad,' said Mavis. 'Not like being a foster-parent. You can take him away for the odd weekend if you like, but that's entirely up to you. You don't have to sign nothink.'

'In that case I take it as a great compliment that you should ask me,' I said, and meant it.

'There ain't no one else I'd rather have,' replied Mavis. And I knew she meant it.

The Bodyguard

Last night, after I locked up the park, I took Mavis for a drink and a game of darts in the Leopard. It is a very old, grimy pub hung with cobwebs, and most of the customers are dossers and renegades who have been barred from all the other hostelries in the nearby City Road and Central Street. One of the main attractions of the place for me is the personality of the landlady, Doll, with her soft white hair braided on top of her head, her neat little gold-rimmed spectacles and print dresses. She must be in her seventies, and she always looks so prim and lady-like that it was quite a shock at first to hear her telling a tiresome regular to 'Ferk orf, there's a good boy'. Even the most hardened and drink-sodden men are somewhat cowed by Doll, and when they are told to leave they go without questioning her judgement. A small and extremely savage Yorkshire terrier barks and nips their ankles to make sure they go on their way quietly.

Doll and I have something in common—an excess of tolerance. Her pub is full of the rejects from adult society; and the unwanted, lonely and difficult children come to my park. She always fusses over me, and last night was no exception. Without even being asked she made Mavis and myself two bulky beef sandwiches and put a large jar of pickled onions on the bar between us. She knows I have a particular liking for them and never seems to mind how many I eat.

'That'll be eight-and-six.' Doll has an utter contempt for decimalisation and for most things modern. 'Just finished?' she enquired amiably as I was frowning over my ten and five pence pieces in my efforts to translate them into old money.

'That's right, Doll.'

'Now you mind how you go home. It's getting really bad along the City Road.'

At that moment six youths of about eighteen entered the pub. They had come to play table-tennis in the back room. They nodded at me shyly and went up to the bar. The gang were all dressed identically in black satin-look zipped jackets and tight black trousers. They looked sleek and lithe as cat burglars. A couple of them had dyed red and orange streaks in their hair and they nearly all wore one small ear-ring in the left ear.

'Blimey,' said Mavis. 'I wouldn't like to meet that lot on a dark night.'

'I do. Frequently.' I stabbed the fork into yet another pickled onion and reflected that I really must bring a jar in soon as I was eating Doll out of house and hostelry.

Mavis stared at me incredulously. 'You know 'em?'
'They're my protectors. My bodyguard.'
Doll leaned her arms comfortably on the bar and regarded me fixedly. 'Go on,' she said.

I told them about the night I had shut the park and walked briskly down the narrow, ill-lit alley leading into Central Street. Three of the gang had appeared from nowhere and taken up a position on my left and just ahead of me. I pretended not to notice as they kept pace almost beside me, but, as the cockneys say, it certainly 'made my bottle twitch'. Then another three had crossed the road and fallen in step just behind my right shoulder. I had never felt so surrounded in my life and could not work out what they wanted. The most disconcerting thing was that they did not speak, and their bizarre appearance made them look like something out of 'Clockwork Orange'. And so, with three of them in front of me and the other three dogging my footsteps, we proceeded down Central Street and along the City Road.

There was hardly anyone about at this time of night but, oddly enough, I did not feel threatened; simply puzzled. I kept wondering if I should say anything to them, but decided to let things take their course. When eventually I arrived at my bus stop they stood on the corner a few yards away. One of them started nonchalantly cleaning his nails with the tail of a steel comb. Another kept glancing over in my direction. They were all standing around in postures of stylish languor yet vaguely threatening trouble for anyone who might dare to accost them.

I grew tired of waiting for the unreliable bus and, weary after a thirteen-hour day, decided to hail a cab. I put out my hand a few times but most of them were already hired and the others pretended not to see me. At length, one of the gang let out an ear-splitting whistle and flagged down a taxi on the other side of the road by frantically waving his arms and jumping up and down. The driver turned round in the busy, badly-lit street, probably privately cursing to himself. To my surprise, the one I assumed to be the leader bent forward and opened the door, beckoning me over. Underneath the street lamp I could see the bright splash of pink in his fair hair.

'Thanks.'

'Good night, keep.' He grinned at me, and I watched the six of them loping off up the road, stark black shadows beneath the imposing block of the Kestrel House skyscraper.

The next day again I had to work from eight in the morning until nine at night as Nola was off sick. It was during the school summer holidays and towards the end of the day I felt punch-drunk from exhaustion.

Wearily, I wended my way into the Leopard, and as Doll was busily and beautifully attending to the froth on my draught Guinness with a knife, the gang walked in.

The leader came and stood at the bar beside me and ordered six shandies. Perhaps they were younger than they looked.

'Why did you follow me last night?' I asked him.

'We wasn't following you.' He flicked the rose-coloured cowlick out of his eyes and gazed at me steadily. 'We was just walking you to the bus stop.'

'Yes, but why? I don't know you. I never saw you before last night.'

'Yeah, but we know you.'

He was incredibly shy really and stared down at the tattoo marks on his fingers—TRUE LOVE.

'Me little bruvver goes in your park,' he said at length.

'And your friends over there?' I gestured towards the five around the table-tennis table.

'Their little bruvvers and sisters go in your park.'

'I see.'

He sipped at his shandy, still with eyes lowered.

'Your ol' man don't come down to meet you, does 'e?'

'He does when he can but he's often working late, too.'

'Yeah, well, like I say, we'll walk you to the bus stop, and if you get any bovver in the park tell 'em the Marshes will take care of 'em.'

'O.K.,' I said. 'And thanks.'

Doll and Mavis had listened intently to my account. 'That's very interesting,' said Doll. 'I remember when I was a girl there used to be a lot of gang warfare around here. The small shopkeepers and publicans used to pay protection money to one gang leader so they would not be attacked and robbed by another lot from over the other side of Hoxton.'

It was strange how customs and traditions survived, but then I was very near the East End where people have always had to fight for a peaceful existence.

'They've never asked me for anything.'

'They wouldn't, because you pay them in kind. You are protecting the little kids, their relations, so it's only natural that they see you all right.'

As I rose to go that evening the Marshes left their game to escort me on my way. Although their conversation was mainly conducted in monosyllables I was growing quite attached to them.

One mention of their name in the playground provoked more fear than the sight of ten panda cars. I only wish I could have taken them with me later on when I was transferred to the New North Road. I needed them there.

Martin, Sheila, Tom and Gerry

Many sociologists have written about high-rise flats and what they are doing to people. I suppose their worst aspect is the depersonalisation of the individual.

A beautiful early Sunday morning in October. Pale amber leaves suicide-dive from the trees in the park like Japanese pilots. I have been sweeping up. In the corner of the football pitch I build a small bonfire of the leaves and set them alight. The smell is exquisite combined with the aroma of two fat rashers of bacon I am frying in the hut. I feel rather like a gypsy and very rural in spite of the concrete.

Martin comes in to see me and I can tell he is in a bad mood. His feet shuffle sulkily in the old plimsolls. When he shuffles instead of walking I know we are going to have problems.

Martin suffers from the high-rise syndrome even though he doesn't know it. He glares at the smouldering leaves. 'Why didn't you let me do that?' Kicking the pile so that small sparks scuttle away like beetles struck by lightning.

'Didn't think you'd be around. Thought you'd be in bed.'

There are times when I positively resent the intrusion of another person. This was one of them. Without giving him a backward glance, I walked over to the hut and examined my breakfast which was turning deliciously brown.

Martin, as I expected, came and stood at the entrance to the hut, leaning on the lower half of my stable-like door staring at me myopically through his big black spectacle frames.

'Piss off, will you? This is my breakfast.'

I looked with lust at the pile of unopened newspapers—*Sunday Times, People, Observer, News of the World*. Why the hell did he always have to appear first thing Sunday morning? It was bad enough having to work on a Sunday without having breakfast and a browse through the papers disturbed. I really did feel resentful towards him.

'Come back in half an hour,' I said. 'I just want a bit of peace.'

'O.K.' He slid away moodily. I cut a tomato in two halves, dropped them in the pan and glanced back at Martin retreating across the playground with his James Dean gait, slouched shoulders, hands in pockets, legs thin in drainpipe trousers, feet interminably dragging. 'Thank God for that,' I said aloud.

Five minutes later I was sitting, contemplating my plate with pleasure, the *Sunday Times* colour supplement propped up by the milk-jug. Reappearance of Martin.

'Look what I've found.' He held a dead pigeon over the door, dangling it by its legs.

My knife and fork dropped with a clatter. 'For Christ's sake,' I shouted. 'Take that disgusting thing away!'

He stared at me idiotically. Sometimes I wonder whether he is mentally retarded. 'What do you want me to do with it?'

'Just get it out of my sight. Bury it.'

'Can I have the spade?'

'Take it. Take anything.'

I watched him reach in for the spade and drag it noisily clattering against the concrete over to the trees by the slide. I turned back to my plate not feeling nearly so hungry.

Five minutes later I was half way through my meal when Sheila appeared at the doorway, pale-faced, tight-curled, fag in mouth. She was another of the mothers who came to the park, and I'd heard a lot about her sex problems.

'You know that stuff you got me.'

'Yes?'

'Well, we tried it last night and it didn't hurt one bit.'

(She was talking about K.Y. As her sex-life had been far from satisfactory, due in part to a sterilisation op., I had advised her to try a lubricant. She had not known what I meant so I went down to a chemists and bought some K.Y. It just so happened that my 'present' coincided with her wedding anniversary.)

I did not feel like discussing last night's antics over the bacon and eggs.

Sheila pushed open the hut door and stood inside. 'Can I come in?'

'You are in.'

She settled herself in the armchair and poured herself a cup of tea. I tried to concentrate on my food.

'I put it on him.'

'Did you, now?' Savagely, I sliced into a piece of toast.

'Yeah. I pushed back his foreskin and rubbed it in. He quite liked that. Said that it interfered with his coming, though. I did like it though. Made no end of a difference. It was all nice and slippery.'

The toast began to taste like clay.

'I'm going to tell everyone about it. It made no end of a difference.'

'So you said before.'

Wearily, I pushed the plate into the middle of the table.

'I'll send all my friends down to see you who have them sort of women's troubles.'

Some tea from Sheila's cup slopped all over the pretty fashion model in the colour supplement.

'My talents are wasted,' I said, sarcastically. 'I ought to run a sex shop.'

'You don't eat enough. That's why you're thin. Don't you want your breakfast?'

'I was trying to eat it.'

Unperturbed, Sheila chattered on, telling me with evident pleasure about the misfortunes of her neighbour who had just received an eviction order. 'And she can't work because she's bleeding internally and waiting to go in for a scrape. One of her tubes is blocked.'

I watched the eggs congealing on my plate.

'If you don't get a scrape you get cancer in the womb. Did you know that? A terrible discharge she's been having, poor girl. Looks like cottage cheese.'

I studied the milk-bottle, wondering about a cup of tea, but the milk looked murky and somehow indecent.

Sheila continued to babble on inanely, the subjects ranging from last night at Bingo, her husband's sexual prowess (a different 'high-rise' syndrome), what she bought at the jumble sale, to the malfunctioning new colour-TV. I tried to stifle my yawns. I am sure I invariably said 'no' when I should have said 'yes', and vice versa. When I am bored I always do this. The talker has to be very insensitive not to notice.

At length, mercifully, Sheila went off to relieve herself. I scraped the remains of my disastrous Sunday breakfast into the dustbin. From the lavatory I heard a scream. Sheila came running out, nearly tripping over her fluffy pink slippers.

'Go and see what's down the fucking toilet.'

With some trepidation I followed her, glanced briefly down into the pan, and was nearly sick. Dead animals or birds have always repelled me, and the shock of seeing a dismembered pigeon's head was too much on this beautiful October morning. I dreaded to think where Martin had scattered the other parts of the bird's anatomy.

Tom and Gerry came into the park. I was so delighted to see Tom that I nearly ran and hugged him. He is a boy of thirteen, gentle and sensible and really very intelligent. His face is very lovely with rosy cheeks and big blue Irish eyes, like a pre-Raphaelite child. He has shoulder-length brown hair, always gleaming and clean. In spite of all the bad influences of the Barbican he appears somehow untouched. I feel protective towards him and keep a close eye on the company he hangs around with, mainly a gang of little thieves. At first I thought he was a strong enough person in his own right to be above their corrupting influence. Later I was proved wrong. I had reckoned without Gerry, a small boy with a dirty face and braces on his teeth. Gerry comes from a generation of thieves and his real name is Colin but as he and Tom are always together they have been nicknamed after the cartoon.

'Tom,' I said. 'Martin has gone and cut a dead pigeon up and left bits of it all over the place. Please help me. You know I can't stand anything like that.' Tom knew very well.

We are always playing chess and sometimes he deliberately lets me win by throwing away a queen. I am always telling him to find other partners. I taught him the game, and my style is building up a very strong defence wall and letting my opponent think I am giving away pawns *ad infinitum*, when in reality my key pieces are castles and knights. I am not very good but it is my own original style and has a certain deviousness which tends to throw more experienced players. Unfortunately, Tom has imitated my methods. It is flattering, but our games go on for hours.

Tom carefully scouts around, tactfully not showing me his gruesome finds. In the meantime I make another pot of tea and feign disappointment when Sheila tells me that she has so much to do that she really must be getting along. In her own way she is very good-hearted. No one can be blamed for being a boring conversationalist if their life is so drab. I have suggested so often that she takes a part-time job, but I think she genuinely does like being a housewife. The housekeeping money her husband gives her is invariably spent on the four kids, who are already having extensive treatment for dental decay. I hardly ever see one or other of them without a sticky lollipop or a Jubbly or chocolates clasped in their hands or bulging in their cheeks. Sheila tends to over-indulge them in some ways so that they are almost beyond control. I do not feel that they get enough love. They get plenty of kissing and cuddling, but not much real, understanding affection.

Tom is starved of affection. Why else does he keep coming to the park to play chess with someone over twice his age?

'You had yer breakfast, keep?' he asks now in a concerned way.

'Not really, Tom. Certain things put me off.'

'I'll go down the Chink takeaway later if you like.'

'That would be very kind.'

He is already setting up the chess-board with the white pieces towards me.

A Voice from the Past

Whenever the telephone rings in the hut it makes me jump. Whoever would want to telephone me, anyway? Very few people except my nearest and dearest know where I am. I have deliberately cut myself off from my previous existence and all the phoney acquaintances I made during that time. It rang this morning.

I was amazed to hear a rich, plummy voice: 'Gill, *darling*! What on earth are you doing with yourself?'

It was unmistakably an employment agency voice, but whose? The curious thing was that nearly every one of them sounded the same and when I had been in that world I had not really noticed. In fact I had probably talked in the same affected way.

'Who is that?'

'Phyl-lis. Surely you remember me?' drawled my 'friend'.

'How ever did you get my number?'

'I was very concerned about the way you simply *van-*

ished. *All* the girls were very *cur*ious, so I rang your father and he told me you were working in a *park*, of all places! Is that really true?'

'Yes,' I said, enjoying myself immensely.

'But *dar*-ling, how *could* you?'

'Oh, but I can.'

'But whatever do you *do* there?'

'I spend most of the day playing chess or reading, pushing babies on swings, putting T.C.P. on grazed knees and making tea for the mums. I also sweep up the leaves and burn them and clean out the lavatories.'

'Good *hea*-vens!' I heard her take a deep breath.

'I'm very happy.'

'How absolutely extra*ordinary*; but then you always were a most un*usual* person. But how could you de*grade* yourself in this way?'

'Degradation is all in the mind. Personally I find the business of selling people far more degrading. I only wish I'd seen the light before.'

'But you are so completely *wasted*! There's a super job going for a Branch Consultant at five thousand a year. That's why I rang you.'

'You haven't told them about me?' A hard edge crept into my voice.

'But of course, dar-ling. We girls must stick together. In fact, one of the directors will be ringing you this afternoon.'

I was filled with an irrational rage.

'Phyllis, do me a favour. Please tell him I do not want to know. Tell him I'm quite happy with my forty pounds a week and my peace of mind. At least I don't feel ridden and pressurised. I can sleep at night and I rarely drink anything stronger than Guinness. I don't need the people who seem to need me so much. And please don't give my 'phone number to anyone else.'

'*Dar*ling, are you quite sure you have not gone completely *mad*?'

'No. I've never felt saner in my life. I appreciate you trying to help me, but good-bye, Phyllis.'

I left the telephone off the hook and strolled out into the sunshine. It was only about nine o'clock, so I sat on a bench throwing bread to the birds and watching the little worried people hurrying past my park on their way to the City.

Alf came and perched on my shoulder and gave me a very wise look.

'Maybe I'm crazy, but out there some of them are mad as hatters. Don't you agree, Alf?'

He nuzzled my ear with his beak and I pushed him away a little roughly as he was none too clean and probably crawling with fleas. There was something symbolic about the disdainful way he watched the other pigeons fighting and scrapping savagely over the last remaining crumbs.

'We're two of a kind, Alf,' I thought. 'Both of us are loners. Let them all get on with it. We will sit back and watch them hang themselves, stab each other in the back and hoist themselves with their own petards.'

The entrance of Mavis and Robert interrupted my reveries.

'Wotcher, cock,' she called.

'Hallo, poor dog.' Robert came running to me, arms outstretched.

I love you both, I thought.

Ruthie

Today is the sort of long, lonely Sunday when I feel as though I am manning a lighthouse instead of keeping a park. There has been a violent storm, which was rather exciting as I sat huddled in my little hut with the thunder crashing around me and the lightning eerily flashing yellow and purple around the high-rise flats.

A violent day in a violent district in a violent city.

I have seen a couple of rather strong films just lately: *Taxi Driver* and *Helter Skelter*. The latter was really very horrible but some compulsion made me go on watching even through the most brutal and blood-sodden scenes.

Brian is convinced that I get pleasure and enjoyment out of such films. I suppose in all honesty there is an element of morbid fascination in my cinema-going tastes. We are going through a tough time, when the young feel negative and neglected even though they are materially more prosperous than previous generations.

Tom and Martin seem surprised that they almost always find me with my nose stuck in a book. Reading seems to be an alien pastime to them and many others. Television has taken over in most homes and many times I am excluded from conversation because I do not have a 'box'. I am unable to join in discussion about 'Charlie's Angels' or 'Coronation Street'. Kids stare at me oddly when I say I have no set. Their general reaction seems to be that I must be very poor indeed. The people of the Barbican are so generous that they keep offering me second-hand sets, which I have to decline.

I am surrounded by reminders of their generosity. When I look around the hut I see that Cathy brought the cups, Martin the tea-bags and Mavis the salt-and-vinegar shaker for my fish and chips. I am wearing a pair of shoes that Margaret gave me and and an old anorak of Tom's over my denims.

To refuse to take these things would hurt these people, so I merely thank them and wear whatever they give me, or put it on prominent display. I do not think they really believe I am hard up. To them I represent a kind of confessor, marriage guidance counsellor, sympathiser and friend. These constant little gifts are just their way of saying 'thank you'.

Ruthie runs to the hut, rain in her lank hair, a battered coat over a short summer dress, and holes in her plimsolls.
'For God's sake, child, get in there!'
She is choking with tears and hardly able to speak. I dry her hair and make her take off her socks, plimsolls and coat, lending her one of my overalls, and she huddles by the electric fire, her feet on a cushion.
'It's me dad,' she chokes.
'What about him?'
''E 'it me mum an' 'e went for me. Now 'e's gone down the pub. Fucking bastard.'
Ruthie is only nine, and she would be better off in care. She stuffs a fist in her mouth to stop herself hiccuping with sobs.
I make her some hot sweet tea and let her talk and I listen until she has relieved her feelings. Afterwards, I pick up a book and read her a story about a giant crab, translated from some Indian tales for children. The fire is very warm and she drops off to sleep with her head against my knee.
After the pubs have closed her father comes into the park to collect her. His face is very red and he sways slightly. Incongruously, in his arms he carries a fat pink teddy-bear which he has won in a raffle. He belches and grins. 'Ow yer doin', mate?'
'O.K.' I gaze at him distantly.
Ruthie wakes up and when she sees him starts to cry again.

'Look what I've brought me lovely kid, me beautiful girl, then.' He sits the bear absurdly on his shoulder.

'Fuck off, dad,' Ruthie says wearily, but she picks up her still damp coat. I help her put on her plimsolls and socks. She clings to me.

'What's up wiv 'er? Who's daddy's girl, then?'

Without a word she gets up and walks out with him, but when he tries to hand her the bear she pushes his arm away with a surprising strength and roughness.

Transferred Again

It is September. The other morning Mavis and I were sitting in the sun feeling on top of the world. I was attempting to teach her to play chess, but she had been so used to draughts that she kept jumping diagonally over my pawns and trying to take them. Eventually we collapsed with laughter.

'I ain't arf dozy.'

'No, you're not. It's just that you've hardly begun yet. Besides, it's too hot.'

The foreman came in riding a bicycle and greeted me with a grin. 'How you doing, then?'

'O.K. Look, I need some more first-aid kit. We're running low on bandages and T.C.P. and . . .'

He cut me short.

'Never mind that for the moment. I've got something more important to ask you. How do you feel about a transfer?'

'Where to?'

'Oh no! You can't take 'er away from 'ere!' Mavis looked really upset, and she can be very outspoken.

'Not far, Gill. Just down the New North Road. I've got a little bit of aggro down there. Nothing very much, but the kids are on the rough side, and I think you can handle them.'

I was very loth to leave Nola and Tom and Martin, but I was flattered, and although my protectors saw me down the City Road it still took me an hour sometimes to get home, and Tufnell Park was decidedly dark and dodgy at night.

As if he could read my mind the foreman told me that the new park was directly beside the route of the 271 bus, which stopped almost outside my front door.

'Do you have to know now?'

'I'm afraid so. I need a replacement right away.'

Feeling vaguely disloyal I muttered that, yes, I would take it, and he patted me on the head and looked pleased.

I was glad that Mavis had been a witness because when Nola came on duty that afternoon she looked very miserable when I told her the news. 'Jaysus, an' we were gettin' on so well.'

'I know, Nola. I was in a very difficult position.'

'She didn't 'ave no say in it 'ardly. It was all of a sudden like,' Mavis affirmed loyally.

'I wouldn't like you to think I put in for a transfer. The foreman just came and said he needed me. I've loved it here but I have a terrible transport problem at night and I keep getting accosted along Holloway Road.'

'I'll make a pot of tea,' announced Mavis tactfully.

Nola needed a lot of consolation before she could see my point of view and I had to reassure her repeatedly that if it had been left to me I would never have contemplated a move.

Tom and Martin took the news far more calmly.

'That's O.K., Gill. Wherever you go, we'll go.'

I laughed and started to sing 'Me and My Shadow', and Tom and I camped about doing a sort of tap-dance.

'Christ,' said Martin. 'What talent!'

'A landlord once offered me the job of emptying his pub at closing time.'

'We can quite see why.'

After we had all exchanged a few dirty jokes we decided to have a game of rounders. Mavis got very hot running around and giggled while her large bosom shook, and Tom had to keep climbing on the roof next door retrieving the ball, because I tend to bat rather violently. Martin set fire to the dustbin because he enjoyed jumping in it to put it out, and Nola sat having a glass of stout in the Leopard and getting maudlin. 'Oi'll never find anyone else who'll put up with all me little idiosyncranasities.'

'With yer what?' asked Doll, astonished.

'I'm a divil with me words. It always makes Gill laugh.'

This conversation was reported to me later that evening. 'She was really cut up, the poor thing. In fact, we're all very sorry to see you go. I was wondering if we was to get up a petition . . .'

'Doll, please do me a favour. No petitions, please. With the reputation I've got the Council would most probably think I incited it.'

If Nola could have seen that 'park' down the New North Road she would undoubtedly have crossed herself and said a dozen Hail Marys.

I walked straight past it the next morning, giving it barely a second glance. It was only when I got two hundred yards down the road that realisation slowly began to dawn and I retraced my steps. There were no trees at all and it was so tiny that it looked like somebody's back yard. It was actually on a building site where they were constructing council flats and it was fenced by bits of tin and one crumbling wall; a little pocket handkerchief of concrete with one roundabout, a slide, a see-saw and eight swings, all needing a coat of paint.

The hut was very small and battered, with peeling green walls, a door which had obviously been kicked in at one time, covered with the scuff marks of hundreds of tiny feet and names and messages carved deeply into the paintwork: CAROL IS GREAT and WAYNE 4 DEBBIE.

Beside the hut stood two large tin boxes which looked like cupboards. I wondered if they were sort of temporary sheds for deck-chairs and gardening tools, although what exactly you were supposed to dig up here was anybody's guess. As I moved closer I saw the word TRANSLOU printed on each door; so, at least I had my convenience near at hand. In fact, with all the excitement, I felt a burning need to relieve myself immediately.

I unlocked the dingy little hut and hunted for the keys of the lavatories, as they were both locked, but my search proved fruitless. Hopping on one leg I glanced anxiously at my watch and saw that it was only eight-thirty—and the foreman did not normally call round until at least twelve o'clock. I was too shy to go and ask to use the lavatory on the building site, and feeling desperately uncomfortable I decided to use a yellow bucket which I found at the bottom of a cupboard. To my dismay I found that the infernal hut did not bolt from the inside and so standing on one leg like a stork, with my foot pressed against the door to stop it flying open, I proceeded to go about my business. Crouching down is a mere feminine convention—necessity is the mother of invention.

I was in the middle of blissfully though awkwardly urinating when a loud voice outside boomed: 'Top of the morning to you!' Christ! What on earth was the foreman doing round this early?

'I'll be out in a minute,' I yelled.

'What you shut in there for? You're not ill, are you?' He sounded concerned.

'No. It's just that you couldn't have come at a worse moment.'

Thank heavens he got the message for he let me finish my pee in peace and when I emerged, red-faced, he was doubled up with laughter.

'Can I please have the key to those confounded things?' I snapped irritably. He handed them to me.

'I nearly didn't find the place,' I said crossly. 'You didn't tell me it was like this. What a dump!'

'I'm sorry about that. I came early to see if you'd settled in all right.'

'What a bloody travesty of a park!'

'Now calm down and don't get so excited. It's only temporary until they finish those flats, and somebody has got to work here.'

He could have put it more tactfully. Although I liked the man I did rather feel as though I had been taken for a ride.

'Well, find yourself some other mug, or I'm getting on to the union.'

He patted me on the head, which is a habit that normally endears him to me but which today I found infuriating.

'If you can't settle in down here,' he explained patiently, 'and really feel unhappy, well then of course I'll move you, but I have a feeling you'll get to like it here. Please give it a chance. You got on well with the kids on the other park and this place needs someone like you. Just give it time.'

He made me feel that I would be doing him and the community at large a gigantic favour, and I found that irresistible.

'O.K.,' I said. 'You win. I'll give it a bash.'

He smiled. 'See you on the roundabouts.' This was his own special parting phrase. Another habitual saying of his was: 'Worse things happen at sea', whenever I showed him broken windows or a wrecked swing-seat.

I found a tatty old deck-chair and took it outside the hut and started to read *Catch 22*.

I became so deeply engrossed that the arrival of Nola two hours later made me jump with surprise.

'Jaysus, Mary and Joseph! Whatever is this place?'

'You may well ask.'

'What did they want to take you away for? Oi've got one of them temporary students sent to keep me company. All full of grand ideas about child psychology and social reform. He's talking away at the kids in this refined voice and sure they be laughing at him and his fancy ways. Oi nearly had a heart attack when I went on duty this mornin'. There was a boy with a hammer after smashin' up the bench and this student says to me: "Leave him alone. He's only getting rid of his aggression."'

'Incredible! They'll kill him.'

Nola is staring with some astonishment at the two Translous.

'What the divil be they?'

I decided to have a joke with her.

'They're temporary lavatories. When they're full up a lorry comes and takes them away to empty them.'

'Like prefabs?'

'That's the idea, but they fill up very quickly and so they have to be taken away once a week. On Saturday nights, and brought back Sunday mornings.'

She stared hard at me but my expression remained inscrutable.

I went to put the kettle on and she followed me into the hut commenting on its smallness and general air of neglect.

As we sat in the sunshine clasping our two warm mugs she began to show a motherly concern about the attention I was getting from the half-naked men walking about on the building site. Remarks like 'Hallo, Blondie', and 'Get 'em off!' kept floating over the tin fence.

'You'll be gettin' yerself raped if you don't watch out.'

'Raped? You mean graped. There's at least a hundred blokes in there.'

'And it doesn't worry you?'

'Chance would be a fine thing.' And we both laughed.

'The council might put a cold shower in for you.'

'I'd certainly need it,' I remarked, appraising yet another bare brown torso. 'Mind you, when it's all on tap, so to speak, it kind of turns you off. Brian has spent the last fortnight doing up a nurses' home, and he's been quite subdued.'

A young man came over with a bacon sandwich for me and said I could use the canteen any time I liked.

'County Clare?' Nola interposed.

'That's right, mother.' He looked delighted, and soon they were off on a long discussion about the Emerald Isle and did she remember the Fogartys and the O'Briens? When they had finished reminiscing the young man turned back to me.

'Do you mind if me and me mates comes in here in our dinner-time?'

'To eat your sandwiches?'

'Well, yes . . . and . . .' he blushed with embarrassment. 'We like to go on the swings and things.'

Do men ever grow up?

'All right, as long as the foreman's been. And,' I said, seizing my chance, 'I'd love to have a ride on the dumper truck.' I have always fancied the idea of driving one.

The day wore on and the shadows lengthened. Nola hurried back to see the 'damage' left by her student child psychologist.

The children came out of school and disported themselves languidly, as it was still very hot, on the decrepit old apparatus. Some of them stared at me curiously and I watched them from a distance, feeling that there was plenty of time to make their acquaintance. In my experience, children prefer to make the first approach; they are so often in a make-believe world where it would be sacrilegious to bring them back to reality.

There was, however, a young girl of thirteen, surprisingly beautiful in a fragile kind of way. That rare prettiness which you find exists in the worst slum conditions. Exquisitely delicate coloured weeds stubbornly growing on refuse dumps. She wanted to talk to me and become a friend.

Every movement she made was unconsciously graceful. She laughed, showing tiny white teeth.

She was doing everything in her power to welcome me and make me feel accepted. Her name was Debbie.

Sanctuary

At New North Road there is a continuous thunder of passing traffic—great rumbling lorries sending out acrid fumes as I sit in my little concrete back yard. A far, far cry from the pink and red roses of Regent's Park.

At first I was not at all happy here and one of the reasons is that there is such a lack of privacy. The neat little terraced houses opposite seem to contain a fair number of curtain-twitchers. I am constantly being observed from behind the white net, greying permed heads are continuously popping in and out of the windows. What possible fascination can this stark and ugly little playground hold? They seem to be most interested around opening and closing times, and there is one woman in particular who leans out so far that I expect her to have an accident. I suppose there are people who simply feel resentful about the rising rates and although they have nothing against me personally, I represent the council and if they can find anything to complain about they will.

Today my suspicions are confirmed by the visiting foreman.

'Somebody rung up the Town Hall about you.'

'What on earth for?'

'They said you had dogs in here and a game of football going on.'

'What an exaggeration!'

Three little boys who hardly reached my knees had brought in an old rubber ball which they could scarcely kick because it was so battered and kept deflating. In fact I had tried, unsuccessfully, to patch it together with elastoplast. The 'dogs' must have been a reference to a shabby grey mongrel who crept out of the building site, pathetically searching for scraps of food.

'I can't help it if a ball rolls in or a dog walks in.'
The foreman laughed. 'Don't worry about it.'
'I'm not. It just amazes me how petty-minded some people can be.'
'You must admit you break a lot of rules.'
'I don't break rules. I merely interpret them. Some of them are so archaic and ridiculous that I use my own discretion and common sense.'
'All right.' He could not think of a suitable reply but gave me a conspiratorial wink as he was getting on his bike.
'You know you mustn't cycle in this park,' I reminded him, with a grin.
'Quite right.' He swung himself off the saddle and sedately wheeled his bike out through the gates.
Tom and Martin visited me today.
'God, the wreckers have arrived!'
They proceeded to try and demolish the only remaining brick wall surrounding the park. When I had finally managed to dissuade them from this pastime they came and sat down on either side of me.
'We was only trying to save the workmen a job.'
'Yeah. It's coming down anyway, ain't it?'
Their attention was distracted by the entrance of Debbie in tight shorts and tiny white singlet. They stared at her with ill-concealed admiration but were obviously embarrassed by her beauty, for when she waved to me they looked away. She, in turn, was too shy to come over but proceeded to act very skittishly, leaping about on the slide like a young colt.
Two girls of about the same age and wearing similar

clothes come over and join her. They are both very self-conscious, giggly and aware of their nubile charms, and this somehow spoils them. I suppose Debbie's main attraction is her lack of affectation; the fact that she imagines herself to be rather ordinary gives her this extraordinary charm.

I observe with some amusement that the thirteen to fifteen age group tend to go around in little gangs of two and three and with their own sex. The boys are curious about the girls, and vice versa, but their attitude to the essential difference tends to be of a derisive nature. The boys seem to take a delight in pulling the girls' hair, the girls pretend to wrestle with the boys, then they start to squeal and the boys pretend to hurt them, and so it goes on.

The park is getting crowded because it is one of those marvellous long Indian-summer evenings.

'It's almost home-from-home from the Barbican,' I said, as Mavis trundled in with Robert.

'All you need is Alf,' remarked Tom, thoughtfully.

'I do rather miss him. The pigeons round here aren't very sociable and they haven't got any character.'

'He might fly down,' suggested Martin.

'Don't be so bloody silly,' snorted Tom. ''Ow the 'ell does 'e know where she is? 'E's only a pigeon after all. I can just see 'im walking into the Town 'all and asking where she's been put.'

'We could bring him down in a box,' Martin persisted.

'No. I don't think he'd like it here at all. There aren't any trees and he belongs in the Barbican. He'd feel completely disorientated.'

'Dis—do what?' expostulated Tom.

I explained what the word meant and they listened respectfully. I suppose because they are out of school they do not mind learning. They both have quick, alert minds but do not like being regimented.

We decided to have a game of 'Hangman' and Debbie took Robert over so that Mavis could join in. (I was later to find her an invaluable help with the smaller children.)

When it came to my turn I chose the word 'sanctuary' for some obscure reason. Although they guessed the word while I was still sketching in the gibbet nobody was sure of the exact meaning. Feeling scared of sounding condescending, I explained that it originally had a religious connotation but that it also meant 'a haven, a retreat, a place where animals and people went to be cured, a sort of shelter for those who are escaping . . .'

Everyone was silent, and then Tom murmured: 'You mean like a park. A park is a kind of sanctuary.' He is constantly surprising me by echoing my own subsconscious thoughts. Sometimes I find him astonishingly deep.

After I had closed the park for the day I walked home alone and it gave me time to think. At Mousehole in Cornwall I had visited a bird sanctuary and hospital. The poor creatures that were being cared for were mainly seagulls which had been trapped by the oil which lingered poisonously around the coast. Some of the birds had lost their legs, others were a mass of clogged, stinking feathers. Some were curable, others were not. Yet they were all taken in; something could at least be done to help them.

So many people come to the park carrying their problems with them, their small private wounds. The troubled wives with their bruises, to tell me about the brutality of their husbands. Children looking for somewhere peaceful where they can do their homework away from the television set and the constant family squabbles. At least the park is free.

I have made two new friends in the past week, both of whom are seeking sanctuary and sympathy but for entirely different reasons.

The first is Harry, a traffic warden. He has a round red face and very mild blue eyes behind thick-lensed glasses. He has a very gentle personality and hates booking people, feeling he will never be promoted as he is too 'soft' for the job. 'And yet it is so lovely to be free and to walk about the streets in the sunshine.'

Previously he had been stuck for thirty years as a sales-ledger clerk in the same dreary little office. To his joy, he had been made redundant at the age of fifty and discovered a new lease of life. I knew exactly how he felt and told him about that traumatic day when I had run away from the rat race and into the calm of Regent's Park. Yet Harry has still not quite adjusted to his new profession and cannot bear it when people are nasty to him. 'A big fierce Irishman came at me with a pair of garden shears,' he told me, 'and I'd only asked him to move his van so I didn't have to give him a ticket. He shouted that I ought to be flushed down the 'effing sewers with all the other little rats. He was so very unpleasant and hurtful and I was most surprised the next day when he came over and apologised and offered me a cup of tea. Human nature is wonderful, isn't it?'

'Sometimes,' I commented, feeling cynical.

My other new friend should not really be in the park at all and I have to ask him politely to leave if any children come in.

My first impressions of Luke were most unfavourable because I found his appearance rather frightening. He must be at least six foot two and has a broad frame and very protuberant blue eyes, and he always wears the same black fraying jumper, grey trousers and plimsolls. It is impossible to tell whether he is twenty-five or forty and he has a very disconcerting habit of staring at me continuously without blinking.

The first time he came into the park his silent, staring presence made me so uncomfortable that I came away from my weeding and walked right up to him. 'What do you want? You know this is a children's park.' I spoke abruptly.

'I'm sorry,' he said in a very educated voice. 'I only want to sit here. I'll be quiet. I won't be any trouble. I promise.'

The gentle pleading tone in such contrast to the large bulk of the man somewhat pacified me, but I told him he would have to go if anyone else came in.

Gradually, Luke has started to communicate with me and

the mutual therapy does not seem to be doing either of us any harm. He is, I am not surprised to discover, a mental patient who is allowed out each day but must return to the hospital by seven o'clock at night. He was (again this explains his donnish, preoccupied manner) a university lecturer in the Fine Arts and everything was going well for him until five years ago when his marriage broke up and his wife went off with a younger man, a virile but not academic type. He misses his two children passionately and is still deeply in love with his wife and would forgive her and take her back, but there is no hope at all of a reconciliation. What really unbalanced him most of all was the solitude he had had to endure in the big house, surrounded by memories.

'She even left her clothes lying around . . . but music is the worst thing of all.'

I told him that I experienced exactly the same sensation when certain tunes are played on the radio. I have never been a sentimentalist but whenever I hear Acker Bilk playing 'Stranger on the Shore' it brings back certain blissful beautiful moments in my life with my ex-husband. My guts feel as if they are churning round in agony.

'That's it,' said Luke. 'It twists me in the stomach too. It hurts right here,' and he put his hand in the centre of his rib-cage.

It took time to unclog the oil from the birds' wings at the Mousehole sanctuary. It was not something that could be done in a single day.

The Wonder Drug

The junkies have started to use the park. At least they look like junkies to me. He and she (I think) both have shoulder-length hair, blue jeans and regulation tatty llama coats in which they huddle, shapelessly. Yet there is something more than their clothes which proclaims what they are. The eyes have that wide, hollow vividness, the pupils are over-large. They look as if they do not eat properly or exist on macrobiotic food, and they are not all that young. Probably about my age.

I do not say anything to them at first because they are not doing any harm. Just sitting on the bench and talking, the smaller (girl?) with a forced vivacity, waving her hands about a great deal, although I cannot hear the conversation.

They have not pulled out any needles or rolled any joints, and there are no children in the park, so I simply let them be and carry on reading Sven Hassel; a particularly gruesome satirical war novel, but then I never was a flower-child ... I was born into an age when they were still sending millions of people to the gas-chambers. An age of ration books and powdered milk, evacuation and sleeping in the tube station. I am not like the hippies who want to bury the war and pretend it never happened. I am too interested in reality, even if it includes brutality. The war was shabby, inglorious, pathetic and filthy. Kids today are interested in the war because they cannot remember it, not having been there, and because they enjoy seeing films with bloodshed and sadism.

I look over again at the two on the bench. It is strange. They must be at least thirty to thirty-five. Surely they would remember the sound of sirens? Like me, maybe they were put under the table with the dog and told to wait for the 'All Clear'. I remember hugging that dog, though not from fear. He was large, black and white, a speckled chess-board of a dog. With a sigh, I return to my book.

The smaller (yes it is female!) comes over to the hut. Close to I see that her face is pretty but ravaged with spots all around the chin, probably caused by lack of essential vitamins.

'Excuse me,' she asks pleasantly, 'do you mind if we turn on in here?'

She has taken a tobacco tin out of her pocket and is nervously twisting it around with long nicotine-yellow fingers.

'Sorry,' I say, 'but no. I don't want to turn this place into a kind of Central Park.'

She nods sympathetically. 'Yeah. I see.'

Something in me reacts impulsively. I feel like talking to her. 'Would you and your friend like a cup of tea?'

She looks surprised. 'That's nice of you.'

I plug in the kettle. She shrugs slightly regretfully and tucks the tin away in her jeans. 'Do you blow?' she asks curiously.

'I used to. I don't bother now. Mind you, I have no objection to other people doing it. In private. See, I get young children in here and I have a pretty bad problem with the sniffers.'

'The what?'

'Young kids aged nine to fifteen. They buy Evo-stick and put it in a crisp bag and keep inhaling it. Very dangerous stuff. Can rot the liver and lungs, but mostly I just have to clean up the sick in the john. I worry about them choking on their own vomit. There have been two deaths in Islington already. Directly attributed to glue.'

'God!' she says, shocked by my matter-of-fact tone. 'How awful! I never realised.'

How could you, I thought, when the world you live in is a direct escape from responsibility? Where you only see what you want to see, and sometimes in your hallucinations conjure up visions of non-existent things.

After I have made the tea I go and sit on the bench with them for a couple of hours. I find myself liking them. We discuss the drug scene in depth and they seem surprised at my knowledge of the subject. 'I dare say some very fine poetry has been written under the influence of mescalin, but it just doesn't scan,' I conclude.

Mary, the girl, is very fast-talking and gesticulates a great deal, Andrew is more taciturn, but one thing they both keep trying to put over, as though to convince themselves, is that the use of 'speed' enhances your existence, heightens your perceptions. This argument is getting rather tired, and having worked amongst the end-products of this philosophy I cannot agree with them about the idyllic experiences 'speed' induces.

'How do you know if you've never tried it?' Andrew asks, quite rationally. 'If you've never progressed further than pot how can you possibly imagine the sensation L.S.D. gives you, the awareness of the world around you?'

They actually feel sorry for me because I do not want to experiment. In the past I reckon I messed around with alcohol rather too much. That was a form of escapism too. Now I don't need to blow my mind; I simply enjoy everything the way it is.

'I don't need to try it to imagine it,' I answer.

But they are staring at me in a puzzled way. Maybe they think my old denim overalls belie what I've been saying. They wish to cast me in a role.

'You're into something,' says Mary firmly.

'Yes,' I admit.

I thought of the men on the building site, with their early golden tan, exquisite muscles rippling down their backs and arms, the taste and smell of sweet green things, music over the lake at Kenwood, making love early in the morning.

'What is it?'

'I couldn't really explain.'

'Can't you get it into the country easily?' Their minds are very one track.

'You could say that.' Mockingly.

I am into the Wonder Drug. I am into Life with a capital L.

The Gypsy Cat

She is small and black and resilient. A hardy little bundle of fur whose small pink tongue has removed two saucers of milk and half a tin of sardines with the efficiency of a conveyor belt on piecework.

The fair moved on from Highbury Fields leaving the cat behind them. Three boys found her and were about to throw her in the canal but some other children stopped them. They brought her to me in the confidence that I could solve everything.

'We brought you a cat, keep.'

'But I already have a cat.' A tortoise-shell called Puskus whom I acquired in a similar fashion. She has turned into a very haughty lady indeed and I wondered how she would treat this small, shabby newcomer.

Marjorie looked at me pleadingly through slightly squinting medium-grey eyes.

'But this cat is special, keep.'

'How is it special?'

'Well, you see, it's a magic cat 'cos it's black and comes from the gypsies and it will make you lucky for ever.'

'But where am I going to put it?'

I had nightmarish visions of my tiny flat being turned into a menagerie, stray cats, tame pigeons, all the lame dogs in creation. Throw in a few squatters or Asian refugees in my attic for good measure. The trouble is I am soft when it comes to befriending animals or people who have been cast out from society and this attitude has got me into a lot of trouble in the past. It has made me enemies and lost me friends.

On one occasion I was nearly evicted and had to pay a big bill for damage when I 'lent' a house I was renting to two 'charming lads' from up North. They decided a throw a wild party and there was not one spring left intact on the beds after they had departed.

Dogs I have befriended are invariably pregnant or on heat. Cats tend not to be any too house-proud, especially when I seemed to have a succession of over-zealous landladies forever mopping up and eternally shampooing their Axminsters. And as for people I have tried to help—say no more! I have been robbed, conned, assaulted, taken for a ride in every conceivable way and treated like dirt far too often for comfort.

The cat stared back at me blandly with unblinking yellow eyes from the crook of Amanda's sunburnt arm. It was really very thin. Maybe six weeks old.

'It came out of a caravan,' Marjorie announced proudly.

'I don't care whether it came from Timbuctoo. I just haven't got room for her.'

'Can't she live in the park, keep?'

'Whoever heard of a cat living in a park?'

'Well, you live here, keep.'

With the hours I put in she was practically right!

'Well, I don't know . . .'

I started to stroke the gypsy cat's head.

Debbie

'Come on, Debbie,' I said. 'Let's get away from it all. Let's go up to Hampstead Heath. I'll meet you in the café. You'll see how a real park should be. Untrained. Wild.'

'Is it like the country?' With her deep blue eyes and dark brown curly hair it is extraordinary how beautiful she looks today, wearing her red cap-sleeve T-shirt, small jewels hanging from newly-pierced ears. She has caught the sun so perfectly that she looks as though she has come from the Riviera instead of the New North Road.

'In some ways it's even better than the country. You'll see.'

We took the overhead line from Highbury and Islington station and she sat staring out of the window watching the mean rows of little houses turning suddenly into the leafy greenness of Gospel Oak. We were both reverently struck by the sharp contrast. A ten-minute train-ride separates two completely different worlds.

'This is where all the nobs live,' I said as we climbed out at the Heath.

We walked along admiring the tall white houses, their capacious gardens filled with yellow roses, statues, hammocks, people sipping coffee or Campari on their lawns. Her eyes widened as we looked through opulent windows into rooms crammed with antique furniture and Victorian prints.

I watched with amusement as she stared and stared, occasionally catching her breath with pleasure as she glimpsed the beauty in these other people's lives.

'Oh, Gill, just suppose we lived up 'ere!'

She clung to my arm pleadingly.

'Could we pretend we were rich? Just for one day?'

'I don't see why not. We'll play the pretend-we're-rich game.'

What harm could it possibly do? I was beginning to enjoy the fantasy myself.

'Where are we going now?'

'This is Rosslyn Hill. If I remember correctly there's a beautiful toy-shop down here on the right.'

'Coo!' she exclaimed, and executed a little dance of joy on the pavement. Then her face fell and she looked slightly crestfallen.

'What's up?'

'Debbie ain't a rich name.'

'Never mind,' I said. 'How about Samantha?'

'Yeah, that's all right,' she said slowly. 'But what are you supposed to be?'

I knitted my brows in perplexity. 'I've got it. I'm a kind of rich godmother who has flown over from America,' I improvised. 'I think your little ol' country is just wonderful and your little ol' policemen are just cute.'

She started to laugh and we entered the toy-shop secure in our new roles. Of course all the stately rocking-horses, exquisite dolls and elegant cut-out books were way beyond our means. I felt a strong desire to buy her something without being extravagant so I chose a small red and green brooch which went with her T-shirt, and a pair of scarlet rubber lips which were really revolting but made us both laugh. Outside the shop she shyly pressed into my hand a brightly wrapped chocolate ring which was too small for my finger. (I kept it at home until it melted.)

We walked around a bazaar place with Persian carpets at three thousand pounds a time. The assistant eyed us curiously and was soon trying to interest me in a carpet. I kept up the pretence, trying to keep a straight face.

'Gee! I don't know. I'll have to ask my husband.'

'What does your husband do?' the assistant enquired politely.

'Something in oil. He's out east at present so he might well bring me back a present of one of these.'

Debbie was enjoying the play-acting immensely.

'That carpet ain't big enough, anyway.'

'How d'you mean, Samantha?'

'It's too small for yer living-room.'

I thought we had better make a move. The assistant was staring at us with puzzled fascination.

We found a public house with a garden and decided to sit outside. I bought Debbie a shandy and this made her feel very grown up. 'They'll think I'm drinking beer.' She sat looking sensible and mature and people smiled at us thinking: how nice—young mother with teenage daughter enjoying the sunshine.

Then she had to go and spoil the illusion by producing the grotesque red lips from her pocket, ramming them on and proceeding to drink from her glass, making loud smacking sounds.

'Would you like to go for a paddle?' I enquired anxiously.

'Smashing!' She leapt up, her young limbs twitching for more action, and went dancing out of the garden ahead of me. I gave the locals a friendly grin and they glanced back rather woodenly.

We rolled up our jeans to our knees and paddled around the pool. 'Watch out for glass,' I shouted anxiously.

An elegant old lady stood looking at us.

'Could you please help me?' she asked in imperious dowager tones.

'What do you want?'

'I would like to go for a paddle.'

She had rolled her stockings down to her knees and I helped her peel them over the varicose veins and the stubby white feet.

'Thank you so much, gel.'

Debbie was watching her with big eyes. She had never heard the word 'gel' before.

The old lady stood barefoot, looking rather at a loss as to

how to get into the pond. She seemed very stiff, probably from arthritis.

'You'd be best off sitting on yer bum first, if you know what I mean,' said Debbie.

The old lady laughed uproariously. 'What a splendid idea!' We supported her on either side and sat her down with feet dangling in the pond.

An ice-cream van pulled up and I went and bought three cones with bars of chocolate in them. The old lady looked really delighted. 'You make me feel like a gel again,' she said.

That day, with Debbie, I only felt about fifteen myself. The water felt delicious on our dusty London feet.

'Are you very rich?' asked Debbie, curiously.

The old lady's reply was sad. 'Well, yes, I suppose I am.'

Walking back across the Heath Debbie paused for a moment, looking serious. 'What did you think of that old woman?'

'Marvellous old girl.'

'Yes—but very rich and very lonely.'

I Belong to Islington

I have taken up voluntary hospital work in my spare time. The hospital is only at the end of my road. They asked me if I would like a children's ward and I said, no, I wanted a complete contrast, so I am working two or three nights a week on a general male ward. I do the shopping for the patients and some auxiliary duties like helping to feed people who have had strokes or are frail. I notice how dedicated all the nurses are and the work is giving me a sense of humility. It seems to tie in well with the park. At last, I am part of a community. Previously I felt rather footloose. Now, I actually belong to Islington. I am one of the people of Islington.

Race Relations

Race relations are bad around these parts. Involuntarily I was drawn into a row the other night in a pub where I stopped on my way home.

'How you stick all them spade kids over the park beats me.'

'I don't really notice it.'

'They're all over the bleedin' place. Everywhere you turn. Wish they'd bring Enoch Powell back.'

'Hear! Hear! He knew what he was talking about.'

'Wasn't afraid to speak his mind.'

'You ought to walk around the hospitals,' I say, in the middle of a mouthful of egg and chips.

'Bleedin' wards are full of 'em. White people can't get beds.'

'No. I didn't mean that. White and black are pulling together to save lives. Regardless of colour or creed.'

There is a stony silence and I can feel the hostility in the stares directed at me.

'If they sent 'em back our nurses would get a decent wage.'

I really ought to stop as I am up against a brick wall. This bigotry is impenetrable. Yet I am feeling angry because of the ignorance of the arguments and therefore cannot stop myself.

'Have you ever been round a hospital?' I challenge the

little man in his clerical suit and neat tortoise-shell glasses. 'I work in one and it has opened my eyes. I wouldn't be sitting here now if it wasn't for a coloured person. My appendix burst and a West Indian surgeon operated on me.'

But I can do nothing because this is National Front country, and I feel very lonely and weary after a twelve-hour day on the park.

The little man will not let me alone and the eggs are congealing on my plate and I do not feel like them any more because I took too much brown sauce. Nigger-brown sauce, I thought wryly.

'There's too many of 'em 'ere, though,' he goes on. 'And they breed like rabbits. They'll have to be stopped.'

I threw the knife and fork down and took a long swill of Guinness. 'I hope to Christ you're ill one day and end up in hospital. If you were dying you wouldn't mind what colour hands were easing the pain.'

'I wouldn't have one of them buggers touch me. I'd rather bleedin' well die.'

By now I'm feeling not just tired but curiously frightened. I think of Sharpeville, Southall, the Third Reich and the cattle-trucks passing through Germany and no one bothering to notice, all pretending they could not see or understand.

'You're blind,' I said. 'You're the sort of person who watches Alf Garnett and admires him. He's really taking the piss out of people like you.'

'No need to get nasty.'

'You started it.'

I feel as if the whole brightly-lit room is closing in on me. They are three ordinary, innocuous little men. How can they spit out such vitriolic filth?

They went on and on in similar vein about National Assistance, overcrowding, cooking smells, muggings, free housing and squatting, and I sat there wanting to get away as fast as possible. If these people could have seen the article I had just written on integration for *West Indian World* they might have all turned on me like the Ku Klux Klan conducting a witch-hunt. I had to get out of there.

When I was sitting at home that night I took out a copy of the photograph my friend had taken and given me for the newspaper article. A West Indian family walking along by a boating-lake in some unknown London park. They were all dressed in their Sunday best and had probably been to church. They were holding hands in the way that families do and there was a feeling of unity and harmony about the whole composition. I had thought of a caustic caption: '*Some Muggers Out Looking For Trouble?*' but had discarded this for: '*A Quiet Sunday. Please let's keep peace in Islington.*'

I put Sibelius on my old record-player and lay down on the floor with the cat. I was not altogether happy with the gypsy cat's metamorphosis to house pet. She had pissed all over my manuscripts and I wondered if they were any good after all. Evidently Chockluck did not think so.

However, the soothing quality of Sibelius's Second and the black purring heap around my head made me forget my bitterness for a while.

But when the record finished I did not turn it over; I took Wagner from his old torn cover instead. The savage beauty of Tannhauser was more in keeping with my mood. I listened to the march of jack-boots and closed my eyes and saw flaming crucifixions.

Carol

I have just been telling Carol 'The Story of Flop Leg', a saga about a grasshopper who cannot jump. He meets a ladybird called Petronella who has been abducted from a hedge in Buckingham Palace gardens and is very stuck-up. They take a swan named Cyril along the Thames—Flop Leg lives at Windsor where his father is River Bank Manager—to Tower Bridge. They get transport from a cockney pigeon called Alf—the equivalent of a taxi-driver, complete with meter in his tail feathers and just as mercenary. They arrive home safely in the middle of the Queen's Garden Party and land with great ceremony on a big cake. Alf does the usual thing that a pigeon does. There is great consternation and Flop Leg leaps for his life with Petronella in his arms. He has learnt how to jump and become a hero. The two insects fall in love with one another and live happily ever after. Although they have a 'mixed marriage' they overcome society's taboos and have loads of little hopper-birds who make fine jumpers and enter the Insect Olympics.

Carol sat with a finger in her mouth listening intently while I parodied all the different insects and birds.

'Where did you hear that story?'

'I made it up.'

'Did you really?' Her lips parted, revealing milk-teeth. 'Why don't you get it published?'

'I might one day.'

'I write stories, you know.'

'Do you really? I'd love to read them.'

She looked pleased. Carol reminds me very much of myself as a child. She hates being a girl and is wearing an orange T-shirt stained red with Jubbly juice, old patched jeans, hair cropped like a boy. She is ten, and muscular, and cannot be bothered with her appearance. In a year's time she will change, I am sure. There is nothing masculine about her but she says: 'Boys have more fun. No one cares if they get dirty. Girls and women do all the hard work.'

I can only agree.

The Women

Lonely women are drawn to the park to sit on the benches. Sometimes they do not want any point of contact and sit hunched up looking listlessly into space, not smoking or knitting. At other times they all huddle together in a group bemoaning their lot. I sat with them today and listened.

'I really loved my husband. Found him dead in bed. It was a terrible shock. I was only thirty-four. Well, I had two young children to bring up, didn't I? It took me three years to get over it and then I meets this right bastard. You see my skin? It's very white, isn't it? He was always cracking me one and I used to mark easy. It was really embarrassing as I used to work behind this bar and it was the kind of place where they liked you to wear low-cut things and the customers were always making remarks. "They're not bleeding love-bites, they're bruises," I told them. He got through three hundred pounds of my widow's compensation in six weeks.'

'See that woman walking down the street? Some bugger grassed her up. She was getting her widow's pension and working part-time in the launderette. There's social security spies all round you these days.'

'How can you manage unless you've got two jobs?'

'They're getting up a petition about my little boy in the flats. They say he won't stop shouting and swearing through the letter-boxes. He's only seven and what do they expect, putting young families with kids in with old people?'

'See that girl with the blonde hair just passing the paint-shop? Can't see her getting married, can you? She was always with black men before she met this fellow. He's a respectable man what has a car and has bought her a smashing ring. He puts up with a lot. I think she prefers black to white. I bet you a fiver there won't be no wedding.'

'Whatever you do, don't marry 'em. They always change for the worse, If you live in sin you maintain your dignity, I always say. In fact, you have more, not less security. If he upsets you, you can tell him to get out. Make sure you make a fuss of 'em in bed and feed 'em up, but don't marry 'em.'

'Most men are ponces anyway.'

'You're telling me. All the housekeeping goes down his throat and he pisses it up against the wall.'

'Tried to poison my old man once. Made him a salad sprinkled with cyanide. Thought he'd not notice being as he was so drunk. "This lettuce has got a funny taste, love." "Don't know what you mean," I told him. "The kids are eating same as you." See, I'd made all the plates up separate, but the bastard is cunning and he pushes the meal away and goes outside and spews up, then he comes back and hits me, giving me a black eye. See, I can't win, can I? Thought I was going mad and got myself filled up with tranquillisers but it didn't really help. One night, when he had got really drunk and seemed dead to the world I picked up this hammer. I don't know how he knew what I was at but the sod wakes up! That's poetic justice for you.'

'Look at that silly cow. Thinks she's the queen of the street. Instead of her old man parking his car outside where they live she makes him leave it on the corner of New North Road so's she can parade past everyone. See, it's Friday, and she's had her hair done and she wants everyone to know. A workman had me in stitches last week. "On yer way to the hairdressers, love?" he shouts out at her, when she had just come back!'

'What's so special about her? He's only a lorry-driver.'

'Don't you think my husband would let me out sometimes? I like women's company. I like good old hen-parties and I've never seen a male stripper. I think he imagines we have orgies at them Tupperware do's, and if I go in the local he follows me and drags me out by my hair.'

'Maybe if you got a job you could be more independent, stick your fingers up at him.'

'Give over. I've only just got over a nervous breakdown. If I had to work it would really finish me off.'

'But maybe he's not resentful because you might meet other men, but because it's his money you're spending.'

'Well I earn it, don't I? On my back.'

'They don't look at it that way. They think they're doing you a favour.'

'They're selfish pigs, but what would we do without them? Some of the men on that building site are really beautiful. When I see them all brown and stripped off me pulse rate goes up and I has to take a cold shower. It's enough to give you a heart attack.'

'Women do lust but they're often too ashamed to admit it.'

'The trouble with all this hot weather is that you feel like it all the time but when yer actually get down to it it's too bleedin' warm and you don't really enjoy it. Turns everyone into wild beasts. Look at the population in Africa.'

'Men don't seem to understand that a woman doesn't always want it. They can nearly always do it but we can't. We're not like mentally attuned to it at certain times, I read somewhere.'

'With all this new equality we're still all bleedin' different. Would we like it any other way?'

'I'd like more nights out on me own.'

'I'd like to get out at all!'

'They don't realise. They moan about us sitting down the park all day but look what they spend in the pub!'

'Where else can you go but the park? At least the park is free.'

'Where else can you go when you got no garden?'

'The park is always there.' It was the first time I had spoken; I had been listening so hard.

'It ain't bleedin' free. Look at the rates.'

'Yeah, but the park is always there, like Gill says.'

'So are the fucking rates.'

Rose

Lowry would have loved to paint my park. He would have liked the stark beauty of the building site beside it, the half-finished construction of the four-storey council flats, the big yellow men's toys—the cranes—and my strip of concrete like someone's back yard where the only vegetation that grows are golden-flowered weeds. I never had the heart to do any weeding. The weeds were the only patch of colour in all that greyness. The swings, slide and roundabout have all been painted at one time but now the paint is fading in the long spring sunshine. Most of the people round here look hard. Lowry would have been drawn to their lined, tired, lived-in faces.

He would have especially liked the little boy on Sunday. It was four o'clock and he sat on his expensive red chopper-bike in his tattered shorts, dirty knees and cheap plimsolls with holes in the toes. I said: 'Isn't it time you went home for your dinner, son?'

'Yeah.' He grinned, all long legs and golden-brown freckles. 'We got fish fingers.'

Fish fingers for Sunday dinner! Where have all the traditionalists gone? The trouble is, so many of today's mothers haven't really grown up or accepted their responsibilities.

This came home to me the other night when I walked past the Bingo Hall and saw the women queuing up. I have tried to play Bingo, but it's no good. Not only do I find it a dreary monotonous game, with the inevitable whistles after 'legs-eleven', but I find the caller's tones irresistibly soporific. I try to fill in my book—one is all that I ever dare buy—but find it difficult to concentrate. The inexorability of the number-calling puts me into such a trance that my neighbours get exasperated with me. One or other of them eventually snatches my book to add to her four or five, giving a snort: 'You're goin' to kip, mate.' I watch, fascinated at her skill and powers of concentration. To be able to watch all those numbers at once, without making an error, is quite an achievement. In the interval I promise her ten per cent if I have a win.

'S'all right, love. If you don't mind my saying so you aren't arf dozy. For someone wiv a 'ead-piece you're like a tit in a trance.'

I can only agree.

Rose, one of the mothers who comes into my park, is constantly saying to me: 'When I 'ave a win at Bingo I'll put that down payment on a colour TV.' She is always positive. She is always going to win. I point out that the amount she has spent on the game over the past year would have bought her two television sets. She does not want to know. She must have her infantile dream, the gold at the end of the rainbow. What has she got in the real world? Four demanding, runny-nosed kids all under twelve. A querulous husband who sometimes gives her a crack and has been known to take a strap to his eldest daughter. An overcrowded flat. 'I need four bedrooms. Deidre is getting hairs on her privates. It's not right that she should sleep wiv Johnny. I keep going down the housing . . .' No wonder she escapes to the bright lights and the welcoming arms of Mecca.

The other day, on impulse, she slid down the slide, much to the workmen's amusement. They were sitting on the benches eating their lunchtime sandwiches. 'Nearly split me difference.' She winked at the workmen pointing to a tear in the thigh of her old trousers.

'For Gawd's sake, Rose. Yer putting me off me corned beef.' They laugh uproariously. People seem to look less hard when they are talking about sex. A softness comes to their smiling eyes. Back to the security of the womb.

Last night two men were about to start a fight outside the local pub. A little group stood watching expectantly. I asked what it was about. It transpired that the men were in the darts team and one of them had lent his own personal, rather precious darts to the other bloke's wife as it was 'Ladies' Night'. The husband thought that there must be something in it. 'Yer don't give away yer feathereds for nothink,' he kept mumbling. A big bloke with startling red hair, he kept walking around the smaller man like a large ginger tom stalking a mouse.

I stood watching for a while. The little man had a kind of wiry strength. He lashed out suddenly and caught the tall man in the solar plexus. Somebody cheered.

I decided to move on. I passed my park on the way to the bus stop. The roundabouts looked strangely still in the light from a street lamp.

Basil Brush

Basil has a shock of carrot-coloured hair and rather bulbous eyes, and speaks very slowly and deliberately until he gets excited and starts chattering nineteen to the dozen.

Today he knocks hesitantly on my hut door. 'Hel-lo, keeper.'

'Good morning, Basil. You're looking very spruce.'

Someone has given him a suit they have discarded. It is made of grey flannel but is a little short in the legs and arms so that I can see frayed cuffs and his big feet in white plimsolls and bright yellow socks.

'Can I go on the swings, keep-er?'

'Of course you can, Basil, but you must get off at once if the foreman comes or you'll get me into trouble.'

As a matter of fact my foreman is always in a good mood, being a lovely tolerant man from Somerset. He has found me nursing pigeons with broken wings, and feeding numerous stray cats; once he saw me looking after a big sheep-dog called Lassie who was on heat and attracting a large crowd of admirers even though the council had put up a sign saying: 'NO DOGS ALLOWED'. He just shook his head and pointed a warning finger at me. Another time he arrived when I had a six-month-old baby on my lap and was feeding it from a bottle. The mother was working as a stripper in a nearby public house.

He must know that I am a 'collector' of the downtrodden, the oppressed, the injured and rejected. I feel a certain kinship with him and can sense in him a real love of people, animals and plants—he is a first-rate gardener. Even so, I do not know how he would react to Basil. According to the rule book no one over fourteen is supposed to use the swings or apparatus. Basil must be at least thirty.

I look over at him now where he is sitting on the swings slowly moving backwards and forwards and warbling to himself. Basil has a particular passion for the swings because they make him feel like a bird and he has had a tremendous desire to fly ever since seeing *Peter Pan*. He is smiling as he sings and swings and this makes me smile too. After all, what harm is he doing?

Everything is quiet and peaceful until three boys enter the park. At the sight of the gangling red-haired man in the swing they shriek with delight. 'Look, there's old Basil Brush. Let's throw stones at him.'

Kids are notoriously cruel, and I am very protective towards Basil although he stands a good foot taller than me.

'Piss off!' I shout at the boys. 'On yer bikes!'

One of them stands poised with a stone in his hand and for a moment I think he is going to throw it at me, but my smallness of stature has its advantages. The boys are about fourteen but they are bigger than me, and to attack someone who is little but in a raging temper would look cowardly. To show that I am not scared of them I start walking towards them.

'Go on. Out this park. Don't come back in here no more!'

The boy drops the stone but stands looking at me insolently. 'Give us a wank, keep,' he says, and the other two giggle.

'If you don't piss off out this park you won't have anything left to wank with!' (God, if my mother could hear me now!)

The local idiom apparently works, because one boy says: 'She means it. She's a wild cat.' And they turn and file away sheepishly.

Basil gets out of the swing and comes and stands beside me.

'They don't like me, keep-er.'

'Never mind, Basil. I like you.'

'Do you really, keep-er? I'm making myself some wings and I'll make you a pair and we can fly away together.'

'Great idea, Basil.'

At that moment the foreman pulls up in his white car and Basil slinks out of the gate flapping his arms in imitation of a bird.

'Who be he?' asks the foreman in his pleasant West Country burr, with a resigned expression.

'Basil Brush. He's teaching me to fly.'

'Is he, now?' The foreman pats me on the head in his usual fatherly fashion. 'One thing about this park, I never know what I be expecting to see. Now, about your time-sheet . . .'

Secretly, I think he finds visiting my park quite an entertainment.

Tom

Tom came and spent the day with me and I was pleased to see him because it was one of those interminable rainy Sundays. He is really in trouble this time. Breaking and entering.

'You might get put away.'

'Nah. It's only my third offence.'

'You'll be lucky to get away with probation. What happened?'

'We done this factory. Cogi works on a milk-round so he was able to suss the place out. We took Nippy along with us. You don't know him but he's only four-foot six and a right skinny little bugger. We breaks this window and he climbs through. It's a dawdle. He makes his way round to the back and just opens the door. They ain't got no proper security so it's their own bleeding fault. So we just walk in and help ourselves to a few of them little pocket calculators. They're really neat. Murphy was a bit chicken but he sees this typewriter. Very smart job in a little leather case so we takes that along too. With that story-writing you do, we thought you'd like to buy it.'

'No, Tom, I couldn't touch it.'

'Fair enough.'

'I'd feel like Fagin. You mean you walked out in broad daylight with all this gear?'

'Yeah. We just walked along the street, dead casual. Nobody susses you just strolling along like you own the place. If they see you looking scared and hiding the gear under yer coat, naturally they're going to stop you. Trouble is, we got home safe and I suppose it made us cocky. We stored all the stuff on the roof in Cogi's flats. The caretaker found it,' he finished lamely.

'Well, they pulled me in first, 'cos it runs in my family and I've got a record. Took me down the station but I wouldn't grass me mates up. Trouble is I never reckoned with Cogi—he was shitting himself. Never been in trouble before and he's dead scared of his old man, who's a great big docker. He said afterwards that he had no choice. They promised him a c.d. at most if he give all our names over. Can't say I blame the kid. We ought never to have taken him along.'

Poor Cogi. A bright boy who was always using long words he had just discovered, and drew delicate sketches of field-mice and birds for the walls of my hut. He always struck me as a bit of a loner and I suppose he had joined the gang looking for friends, recognition, acceptance, conformity and glamour.

'Have you got a good solicitor?'

'I've got a solicitor. I don't reckon 'im much. See, the trouble is I'm never at school.'

'What don't you like about school?'

'Mostly I'm bored, bored, bored. Bored out me mind. I try and bunk off everything I can. Know how I got off games? He's a right softie, the bloke who runs games. He asked me why I wasn't going to football and I told him I hadn't got no kit. He asks how that is and I tell him me old man's out of work, me brother's on the dole, me other brother's in the nick and me mum can just about manage to feed us. Daft git only pats me on the head and tells me not to worry. He must be blind! I'm walking about with a new watch on and big flash pens in me pocket.'

'Isn't there anything you like about school?'

'Yeah, there's this right little darling of a teacher. Only about five-foot two with red hair and a beautiful pair of knockers. She's only about twenty-four and her class is always full. Even the girls don't bunk off 'cos she's really something to look at.'

'What does she teach?'

'I don't know what she teaches and I don't care. I go to look, not to learn.'

God help anyone in charge of a class full of Toms!

Colour Prejudice

I ran into a National Front demonstration in Hoxton Street today. Cathy, one of the park mums, had told me that there were platform soles going at five pounds a pair 'down the waste', and I had decided to go shopping. It's only about ten minutes walk from the park.

There was a lot of noise, shoving and ignorant shouting, and I wished I could get away and had never come in the first place. I tried to get past the set, hard, white faces crowding round the man on the platform. Is this what you get for coming to buy some cheap shoes?

'I see that there are all white faces around me. Wise

people. You know what is best for you. Once we have got all the undesirables out of this country we can start to reclaim our heritage.'

A long-haired chap in a donkey-jacket asked: 'What do you mean by undesirables?'

The speaker turned to the heckler, his moustache bristling. Is the resemblance to Hitler intentional? The fawn raincoat has a military air about it. The dull grey eyes look rather dazed and stupid.

'We can only survive by uniting through our pure English stock. Our strength lies in the defence of our heritage, our life blood. Our lost empire can be reclaimed.'

I must get away from here. All I wanted to do was to find the stall that sold the shoes.

'Excuse me.' Two enormous women in head-scarves stood with the stolidity of mules blocking my path with straw baskets on wheels. 'Excuse me,' I said, more urgently. Stubbornly they stood their ground.

A black man came out of a pub. He was laughing over his shoulder at something a friend was saying. He was about thirty-five and very smart in his checked suit with a beautiful arrogant stance.

'Get back, nigger,' shouted a man, and the crowd took up the chant. 'If they're black send them back.'

'Hey—do you mind letting me through?' I stuck one of women in the back quite hard. 'I've got to get by.'

'Who you shoving?' She turned round belligerently. Her eyes looked blurred and slightly drunk.

'I must get through.'

'What for? You came 'ere to listen. You bleedin' well stay. Listen to the man. E's talking bleedin' sense.'

'If they're black send them back,' roared the crowd.

The coloured man stood helplessly, unable to get past the pickets, banners and voices. He did a very brave thing. I am sure he would not have done it under normal circumstances but the tension was too much for him and he looked so alone. He raised a clenched fist and gave the Black Power sign. The crowd let out a great snarl of rage and two policemen came and stood on either side of him.

'I'm not shoving but it's just that . . .'

The two women swung on me vehemently. 'One of them bleedin' commies.'

I was shocked at the violence in the bland, plump faces. How to communicate? 'It's not that. I'm just bursting for a jimmy riddle. I don't want to piss meself.'

The women smiled. 'Sorry, love. Never realised.'

'Why didn't you say so in the first place? Come on, girl.'

Their conspiratorial smiles indicated that I was one of them, and they made way to release me. I lost interest in the shoes. The whole street seethed with hatred. I had to get somewhere where I could breathe.

The next day Angela comes to show me her new school uniform. She pirouettes around outside the hut obviously proud of herself. She is eleven, and has just started in the first year at secondary school. The uniform is grey and red with a very smart badge on the blazer. It is too big for her but she will grow into it, and it must have cost a packet so it is better that way.

'Do you like it?'

'You look really terrific.'

The colour suits her—the soft grey wool against her dark golden skin, the scarlet slide in her woolly black hair. She looks so pretty and innocent.

George and Martin

George is small, wizened and eighty, with a remarkable brain for his age. He used to be a tap-dancer on the halls and can talk back-slang, which seems to be a dying art. He has been in the hospital for nearly a year now and likes it there. He is doing everything he can to stay. Over his bed the staff have written: 'Do not help to feed. Do not help to dress. Do not help to cleanse. Do not help to walk.' They are trying to cure his little cries for help, his child-like efforts to attract attention. He is not really geriatric at all and they keep him on a general ward in the hope this will stop him declining any further.

Martin is sitting outside the hut. He is growing up but still gives way to 'mad half-hours', like trying to ride down the slide on a bicycle or blocking up the lavatory for the sheer pleasure of unblocking it.

'You were very trying yesterday,' I said.

'I know I was.'

'You're lucky you didn't get barred again.'

'I agree.'

'You're funny sometimes, like the time you dressed up in my overall and a wig and stuffed cushions down your front and went down the fish-shop.'

'You laughed about the automatic dustbin opener.'

'That was original.' He had managed to fix it so that every time the loo chain was pulled the dustbin lid popped up.

'But standing on the garage roof and slinging bricks into the playground where there are five-year-olds on swings is just plain daft.'

'I can't help it. I just go mad sometimes.'

'You remind me of George.'

'Who's George?'

'A patient I visit at the hospital. He's just like you only he's old enough to be your grandad. When I go up there he wets the bed on purpose, wants to be fed and sulks if I don't feed him, runs the sister down, and tells tales about the other patients.'

'Sounds a miserable old sod.'

'Apart from that he's a nice fellow. He tries to be as naughty as he can to find out whether I still love him.'

'And do you?'

'Well, I'm the only visitor he's got.'

An Unfriendly Visitor

She is tall, statuesque, wearing tinted frames and an Ossie Clark print, her hair in a long fat gold plait. Her children are called Justin and Jason. Obviously one of your Islington trendies. She strides round my park shrieking in one of those obnoxious, affected middle-class accents—the kind of strident, *nouveau riche* voice which would make anyone with education or real breeding run a mile.

'Not that way up the slide, darling. Come to mummy. He's only a teeny weeny little dog, sweeties, but they do bite little boys sometimes.'

Nauseated, I discard the *Observer* and bury myself in the *News of the World*. Anything to drown that noise. I have just got to a particularly salacious piece when the woman strides imperiously over to me. I look up and smile politely.

'Why are the swings closed?' she demands arrogantly.

'Well, you see, it's been raining.'

'I want them opened.'

I point to a sign:

> THE COUNCIL SHALL NOT BE RESPONSIBLE FOR ACCIDENTS ARISING FROM THE USE OF PLAYGROUND APPARATUS.

'I do try to avoid any danger to the children and, touch wood, I have never had an accident of any consequence.' I am rather proud of this fact.

Print Frock is determined to be nasty. She obviously has a colossal chip on her shoulder. 'I object to paying my rates so that you can sit here reading all day.'

I stare at her, thoroughly confused. How would a woman like this cope with the sniffers, the stray loonies, the cider drinkers, twelve-hour shifts, working Sundays, the danger of being mugged?

She goes on: 'The rates are ridiculous, and we pay for hippie types like you to sit there reading all day!' How nice to be called a 'hippie' at the age of thirty-four!

'Look, love,' I say, lapsing into cockney, 'I knows the rates are high, bein' as I'm a ratepayer too, but I ain't on the bleedin' council. I don't have no say. Why don't yer see yer local MP?'

'I wish I could sit and read all day!'

There is no stopping her and I have to say something outrageous—I am placid until provoked, but then I turn vicious. 'It's better than sittin' 'ere all day playin' with meself.'

This is too much for her. 'Come along, darlings,' she calls to her offspring. 'This isn't a nice little park. We'll find somewhere else.'

Her two stolid blonde children come waddling over. They have self-satisfied, spoilt faces and wide blue, rather stupid eyes.

'I shall be complaining to the Town Hall about you.' The woman can't look at me in the face again. She turns abruptly, and the children trot after her.

'Bring the bleedin' Lord Mayor down for all I care,' I shout at her retreating back.

The Carpet-Sweeper

One of those dark, abysmal April nights. Steady downfall of rain. Sitting miserably in the hut wondering if I could get away with shutting the park at 6.30 instead of 8 o'clock, or will the curtain-twitchers start 'phoning the Town Hall and moaning about their rates? I see no point in keeping a playground open when it is raining, but the ratepayers want their pound of flesh. Some of the people overlooking the park have nothing better to do than look out of their windows and find something to complain about. There seem to be an awful lot of middle-aged women around who only seem happy when they are cleaning, scrubbing interminably, complaining, or just back from the hairdressers.

It is too dark to read properly by the 60-watt bulb. I feel uncomfortable anyway. Supposing the sniffers or the perverts come in?

There is a bang on the battered old hut door with its flaking green paint. I jump and drop my book. Tom, Martin and Steve are standing there looking bedraggled, wet, rebel-without-causish, with their long rain-soaked tresses and black bomber jackets.

They have brought me a carpet-sweeper. They have walked from City Road all along the New North Road in this sudden downpour just to bring me something they knew I needed. I am very touched and make them tea and wax motherly over their drowned-rat locks—why are they not wearing raincoats? Come to think of it I have never seen one of them in a big coat. Perhaps they do not own one between them.

They tell me that they found the sweeper in a derelict house from which the squatters had been evicted. They propose to take it away tomorrow and make it like new. No, they will not take any money off me.

The next day they come back, triumphantly pushing this most extraordinary brilliantly-coloured object. The sweeper now looks like a prop from a pantomime or carnival. Not only have they sandpapered away all the rust but they have sprayed the base gold and painted the handle a bright apple-green reminiscent of the flourescent socks I wore in the fifties, but the crowning glory is my initial 'G' emblazoned an emerald shade on the gold.

'You do spell your name with a G?' they enquire, anxiously.

I am too choked to speak.

'I bet nobody else in the whole of London has a sweeper like that.'

'I don't think anyone has ever had a sweeper like that. Not ever,' I say emphatically.

That night in the little local just off Essex Road they stare at me with bemused expressions as I walk in with my trophy. 'Come to do the cleaning, love?' asks the big blonde barmaid. I proudly show them what the kids have done and they are quite awestruck.

Is this what the sociologists call 'breakthrough'? To me, it is more a gesture of love.

I was warm and glowing inside that night, and it was a lot more than the Guinness.

Paul and Evo

I am beginning to form a strange kind of relationship with the sniffers. It seems to be founded on a sort of mutual respect.

Paul, the leader, saunters into my park. He is followed by a gang of whey-faced smaller boys. They all look high. They are not at the giggling stage; maybe they have passed it. They look strangely disorientated and very tired. They go and sit lethargically at the top and the bottom ends of the slide, gazing wistfully into space. They are between nine and fourteen. They seem to be a new breed of children who never want to play.

Paul is trying to be friendly today. He holds out a greasy bag of chips. 'Here, keep, you want one?'

'Ta.'

Gary is in a determinedly sexy mood. He comes and sits very close beside me and presses his thigh against mine. When I get the opportunity I edge unobtrusively away. There is nothing more asexual than denim leg against denim leg. Lee Cooper cannot turn anyone on. I stopped wearing a skirt months ago when cricket balls kept getting stuck under roundabouts or mysteriously lodged between the loo doors. I had to bend down to retrieve them, and the boys hid them there deliberately.

'Did something bad last night,' Gary nudges me. 'Went down the Sobell Centre but I got chucked out for having too much Evo. I'd met this bird and we went over Highbury Fields. I got really carried away, really passionate like, so I bites off her nipple. You should have seen the bloodbath.'

'Toe it,' yells Paul angrily. He has become very protective towards me just lately. I have taken no notice of Gary but when I reflect that, at fifteen, he is a fully developed man, I do not find this kind of conversation very comfortable. He is obviously trying to shock and I do my damnedest to appear unshockable. Even so, there is something more insidious, more disquieting about him than there was about the Teds who hung around my garden gate when I was fourteen.

Paul senses my discomfort and grabs hold of Gary by the throat of his bomber jacket. 'On yer bike,' he orders.

Gary wanders meekly off, cowed, shoulders bent. Paul is a natural leader. 'On yer bike means "f-off", keep, only I didn't like to say "f-off" in front of you.'

The statement sounds so Irish that I burst out laughing. Paul goes red and surly. 'What you laughing at?'

'I'm sorry. It just sounded funny.'

He leans towards me, lurching slightly. 'Keep, can you smell Evo?'

'Yes,' I said.

'How can I get rid of it? My mum will do her nut and my girl won't speak to me no more.'

'Peppermints.'

'I ain't got no money, keep. Could you lend me ten pence?'

'Yes.' It is so rare for any of them to ask me for money—a fact which at first I found surprising—that I don't begrudge the odd few coppers. (He brought it back the next day as promised.)

'Oy!' he yelled now to one of his minions, a beautiful, delicate child who reminded me of Oliver Twist. 'A packet of Polos, and look sharp about it.' The boy ran off without a backward glance. Surely Paul's leadership qualities could be directed towards some nobler purpose in life than being king of the sniffers?

'See that shop over there?' He points at the little hardware store. 'They won't serve us with no more glue. The Old Bill's been in.'

'The Law were in here Saturday and they asked if I'd

had any trouble. Apparently they set fire to the playhouse on the Packington Estate.'

'Yeah, there was bother over the Pack,' Paul said. This was nothing unusual.

'I might as well be straight with you. If anyone so much as pulls out an Evo-stick in here, let alone sticks it up his nose, I'm getting straight on to the police. I wouldn't just do it, because I never grass anyone up. I'd warn you first. But they have told me to contact them if I see it. After all, it's for your own protection. They know who you are anyway and they know you come in here. I said it was just to sober up.'

'Fair enough, keep,' he said gruffly. 'And thanks.'

The boy came back with the mints and waited politely to be offered one as though he were waiting outside the Head's study.

I looked at the 'bodies' reclining on the slide like fawning sycophants around their emperor.

'Have they been on it all morning?'

Paul nods. 'In fact, the little kids got it for me.'

'Well, you ought to be downright ashamed of yourself,' I blazed. 'If one of them walks out of here and under a lorry in the New North Road what does that make you?'

He gives me a world-weary smile. 'All right. Keep your hair on. I'm not nobody's keeper. They would do it anyway.'

In spite of the tattoos on his hairy arms, the id. bracelet, the leather jacket, the matted yellow hair, the one earring in his big ear, he is only a child—a kid of sixteen. He lost his father just before Christmas and, as the only son, has suddenly had to take on responsibility. This involves working part-time on a building site as well as attending school. I can understand his lassitude and indifference to life. Perhaps he has seen too much already.

'Maybe it helps you to come in here and talk to me. I want you to feel you can, and I won't ever turn you away. I'm not a do-gooder or anything like that. I'm certainly no plaster saint but it's such a bleeding waste, all this.'

I indicate the prostrate forms, the little patch of concrete —our playground—the boring blocks of flats with their doors uniform blue.

'You ever tried Evo?'

'No.'

'Ever took drugs?'

'I used to smoke pot.'

'Do you still?'

'No. I can get high on fresh air and good music. I tried pot when I was about eighteen. To tell you the truth it left me cold. It was hard to get then and you got a great kick out of obtaining it at all. Now it's commonplace. You can buy it on any street corner.'

'What did it do for you?'

'Nothing. That's the whole point. Everyone else was getting this terrific high feeling as we passed the joint round. I felt so silly. These people had asked me round for a Sunday joint, and I was dead green in those days. In fact, I said to mum: "Don't bother to cook Sunday dinner for me. I've been invited out."'

Paul laughs, really laughs. It makes a pleasant change from the inane giggles.

'Well, we were all sitting around on the floor with guitars and people reciting nonsense poetry and passing the joint around, and I was bleeding starving. Everyone started getting very cool and saying how cool they felt and I just felt empty, hungry and worried that I wasn't getting turned on. When you're a kid you hate to be different.'

'So what did you do?'

'I play-acted. I pretended to be high. I looked up at the ceiling and said: "Man!" (Everyone called each other "man" in those days.) "Just look at them little ol' light bulbs." Of course they all stared up gormlessly and pretended to go into a trance. "There's fish coming out the light bulbs. Yellow and purple with great long tails like peacocks' feathers. Man—the colours! They are out of this world!" And I kept on like that for about half an hour.

They lapped it all up. It was difficult to keep a straight face.'

Paul is rolling around clutching his stomach.

'I like your Texan accent.'

'Well, all I could think about was the big shoulder of roast lamb I had missed and I still wanted to keep my self-respect by appearing to be with it.'

We are silent for a while watching the pigeons nuzzling at the discarded chip-wrapping paper. If only they put fish and chips in newspaper like they used to. If only this, if only that.

'Paul, there's something else I want to tell you which is a very private, personal thing but it might help you. My marriage broke up, and it was a long, slow, agonising break-up. I loved him, and I still do, but I was doing a tough job and had accommodation problems. Everything got too much and so I started taking bottles of wine home and drinking them. At first it was decent wine and then as I got more and more hooked it was the rot-gut red biddy. I used to lie on the floor, alone, listening to sad music and drinking myself into a stupor. Somehow I pulled myself out of this state. I was scared of ending up like the dossers under Charing Cross Bridge. Glue and the like never solves anything.'

He smiled at me.

'I'm going home for my Sunday joint. Thanks for the chat, keep.'

He wandered out and his retinue followed.

Death and Martin

'What's up, Gill?'
'Nothing much.' I was pleased to see him today.
'Yeah, there is. Ain't there?'
'Have a cup of tea.'
'Ta.' He took the kettle I proffered and obediently went to fill it from the leaky old tap in the tin lavatory.

He sat on the hut step and looked up at me quizzically. 'Come on. Spill the beans.'

'I was up at the hospital last night and one of my patients died.'

'I see.' Death seems very far away from him; he is not yet sixteen.

'I had taken a bottle of his favourite brown sauce and half an ounce of Old Holborn and I stood there holding them feeling awkward while all the staff did the necessary things. I didn't know what to do with them afterwards so I gave them away to the orderly. I was his only visitor.'

'Never mind, mate. Let me make the tea for a change.'

Martin is growing up.

Basil Brush Again

'It's a pity,' says Basil, 'that we can't fly. Birds can fly. Birds are nothing really. They're just scavengers. They're after yer crumbs and bits and pieces. A bird hasn't got nothing on a man. But a man can't fly. He tries to—like he makes planes and things, but a man's got nothing on a bird. I mean he has to have an engine. You'd have thought man would have learnt how to imitate a bird by now, wouldn't you? I mean he can make like a fish, can't he? He can imitate the movements even though he hasn't got no fins. I mean—a bird's nothing. Neither is a fish, come to that. A bird hasn't got no brain. Well, not a big one, not like a man, has he? If a man can swim he could fly—at least he ought to have got somewhere by now. We can imitate the apes and they can imitate us, and apes are intelligent. A bird's got nothing on an ape. But we don't know how a bird gets those wings of his up, like, and flies. Isn't it about time . . .' and he goes on in this vein for another half-hour.

Two little black boys sit beside Basil on the park bench, staring at him, mouths open, absolutely fascinated.

The Little Mermaid by Hans Christian Anderson lies face downwards beside them. I had been reading them a story when Basil appeared.

Children like their entertainment live.

Paul

I travelled home with the sniffers on top of the 271 bus. They looked respectable and oddly contrite. 'It's nice to see you sober for once,' I could not help remarking. Paul grinned at me cheekily: 'What yer doin' on the bus, keep? Why ain't yer in the park?' 'Being as it's Thursday I finished at three and have been having afters in the Duchess.' They are obviously on their way home from school, hence the absence of Evo.

'Thought I could smell booze. Been on the piss, keep?'

'Guinness is good for you. Glue ain't,' I replied, rather smugly. But at least they could see I was human.

They were fidgeting, restless, with a different sort of high from the giggles, and very friendly. The sun streamed in the top of the bus window and we all looked very brown.

'Anyway,' I said, 'what you doing down the Holloway Road? This isn't your manor.'

'We found a shop that'll serve us. Down near Mary Mags.'

'I get it.' Underneath his suntan Paul was pale and there were rings beneath his eyes. I felt suddenly world-weary and old.

'See yer, keep.' They sauntered off the bus and I watched them go into a little toy-shop-tobacconists. I could imagine the scene inside. Paul saying: 'Why do I need glue? Well, I'm making this model aeroplane like . . .'

There were toys in the shop windows. Games of snakes and ladders. Pogo sticks. Roller skates. A cricket set. A big, furry, yellow teddy-bear. A lump came into my throat and I put on my dark glasses because I did not want anyone on that bus to see my tears.

I remember one Christmas standing in Oxford Street

outside a lighted toy-shop window. There was an enormous furry bear as big as myself that kept jumping out of a box, doing a little dance and waving at the passers-by. It had a silly, ridiculous, lovable face. My marriage was on the rocks. I stood there crying my heart out. Why do things like this affect me so deeply? Death of innocence perhaps. Mourning a childhood that never was, or only briefly. Thank God I had my shades on today. My tears could at least be private.

It is lovely when children can indulge in the luxury of simply being children. Most of the insecurity of adolescence is caused by that horrible in-between feeling. A dread of facing the real world and yet a tremendous desire to be accepted by adults at all costs. What a nasty, difficult, thoroughly unpleasant period—the years between thirteen and sixteen. For a kick-off your body is behaving in a most peculiar way. That awful traumatic business of coping with periods if you are a girl, the breaking of the voice in a boy. No wonder the poor kids are so confused. You only have to look at Colin sitting on the swings, smoking.

We now have a new game on the park called 'Tell Me', and it is becoming very successful. The main reason is that it appeals to all age groups and the big ones enjoy helping the little kids, partly because they can air their knowledge but mainly because it makes them feel more responsible and adult.

A questioner is elected, and a spinner. The spinner operates a little wheel with letters of the alphabet printed round it. When the wheel stops on a letter a question is asked, such as: 'Name a country starting with W.' And whoever shouts 'Wales' first scores a point.

The children's powers of imagination are exercised, and they can be very inventive and amusing. Like the little boy of six who was asked to name an insect starting with the letter N, and said 'Naterpillar', and when the wheel stopped at C, proudly exclaimed 'Clutterfly'.

The older ones are very conscious of themselves and their bodies. I asked Tom to tell me a means of communication beginning with I, where the wheel had happened to land. He looked back at me without blinking an eyelid. 'Intercourse,' he proclaimed loudly. This produced the usual barrage of giggles. I pointed out that the word had more than one meaning, and proceeded to enlarge. With insolent candour Tom replied: 'I am only interested in the one meaning.'

I have made a pact with myself that I will not give in to demands for sweets, bottles of pop or cigarettes unless I am asked politely. The majority of children never ask me for anything so I tend to make spontaneous generous gestures. The temperature the other Sunday was in the eighties so I went out and bought two pints of cockles and winkles and a couple of big bottles of lemonade. They seemed very pleased and surprised and thanked me profusely.

We had a lot of fun digging out the winkles with a pin. I taught them an old music-hall song: 'I Can't Get My Winkle Out', and they were much amused by the *doubles entendres* and went home loudly singing the words. I saw one or two curtains twitch as they walked past yelling: 'The more I try to get it out the further it goes in.'

The Bailiff of Islington's Daughter

Really depressing on the park today. Hardly surprising as I have just come back from the sun-kissed shores of the Isle of Wight. Everywhere looks so grey and desolate and it is very cold for September. Almost cold enough for the seagulls to fly inland. They are much hungrier than the pigeons and swifter moving, streaks of white lightning flashing in amongst the plump, grey, over-fed cockney birds. The building-site men are no longer so brown. They have lost the strut and languid cockiness of their walk. Some of them will be looking for inside work as the winter approaches.

Yesterday I stood looking at a field of gentle cows.

In the little wallpaper shop opposite a sign has appeared:

TO THE SNIFFERS:
WE HAVE RUN OUT OF EVO-STICK
AND THE TILL IS EMPTY.

The old boy in the pub in Sandown. Bert, in his eighties. 'So you come from Islington. How very interesting and historic. Wonder if you know the song, "The Bailiff of Islington's Daughter". We used to sing it at school.'

'No, I've never heard of it, although I've had some experience with bailiffs in my time. Would you mind writing down what you can remember?'

Two boys enter the park aggressively. One dark, one fair. One fat, one thin. About twelve. They peer in at me insolently and then go and perch precariously on the seesaw.

> *There was a youth and a well-beloved youth*
> *And he was a squire's son*
> *And he loved the bailiff's daughter*
> *That lived in Islington.*

Boys' voices shrill on the wind as the see-saw goes up and down:

> 'When roses are red and ready for plucking
> Girls of sixteen are ready for fucking.'

> *Now when his friends did understand*
> *His fond and foolish mind*
> *They sent him to Fair London Town*
> *Apprentice for to bind.*

'Ave yer 'ad it off wiv that Rose yet?'
'Nah. But she lets me put me finger up.'
'They call her the "Easy Rider of Packington Street".'

> *And as he went along the high road,*
> *The weather being hot and dry,*
> *He sat him on a fair mossy bank.*
> *His True Love came riding by.*

The voices sound nearer. This time I am meant to hear.
'Wouldn't mind 'avin it off with that keep Blondie.'
'They say the older ones are more experienced.'
They grind the see-saw up and down in frustration with life in general.

'You see,' said Bert, 'I can't remember the last verse. It was such a long time ago. Would you believe, seventy-five years?' He looks at me apologetically through timid, faded blue eyes, small gold-framed glasses. 'Would you care to imbibe, my dear?'
'Thank you. The same again. I'll go to the local library, Bert, and I'll ask around the borough. I will try and find the music for you.'

'I would be so very interested,' he says, gentle-faced and voiced.

The boys are walking around the park kicking out at bricks which have toppled over from the site.
'If yer ask keep nice she might give yer a 'ard-on.'
'She must get lonely in that little 'ut.'

He smiles benignly at me. 'I would love to visit Islington again. Such happy memories. Long walks with my young lady in Highgate Woods. I was rather a lad in those days.'
Gallantly, because I liked him, I said: 'But you still are!'
He laughs with me. 'We had a house in Canonbury Square with roses around the porch. I suppose it has all changed.'
Bert, if you only knew!

They stop hesitantly outside my hut. I am more than ready for them. I stand up. 'You want to ask me something. Well, ask away.' I move closer, threateningly.
They stammer, stutter, blush, nudge one another. 'You ... er ... got the time, keep?'
'Twelve-thirty. Did you ever sing a song at school called "The Bailiff of Islington's Daughter"?'
Uncomprehending, they stare at me. I am trying to take in their faces. They are round and without the beginnings of hair and their singing is so high-pitched that the voices have not started to break.
'No, we never did 'ear of it. No never.'
'Never mind. I don't suppose you would.'
'Ta ta, keep.' They sling satchels over patched blazers. As they go out of the gate one says, 'This park ain't bad. Thought there'd be an old bag in there.'

I pick up the postcard of Tower Bridge and write to the dear old gentleman, Bertram, my friend, care of the Stag Inn, Lake, Sandown, IOW.

Dear Bert,

   I am trying to trace your song and will get no rest until I succeed.

   The weather is up and down like Tower Bridge but I hope you're in the pink.

   London is still the same as ever and I walked through Canonbury Square and saw the early Autumn roses round the porches and thought of you.

   It was lovely making your acquaintance and I'll see you next year.

Love and kisses,
Gill

Susan and the Soap

Susan is backward. She is eleven years old but has the mentality of a child of six. Her speech is slurred and baby-like so that at times she sounds like a drunken three-year-old. She brings me a drawing of houses covered with kisses and her name written unevenly across the bottom left-hand corner in bright red.

She stands by the hut door with her thatchy yellow hair, her big blue vacant eyes and young-old face. She is very dirty today and smells of stale urine. The other kids ostracise her and call her 'Smelly Susan'. One day, a woman, out of kindness, gave her a bottle of cheap perfume and she drenched herself in it and kept refilling it with water from my tap. She is wearing a sequined sweater with green paint on it, one of her mother's skirts, and the same scuffed brown shoes she has worn for the last year. Whenever I see her I am filled with anger, even more than pity.

   The family is quite well off. The other three children are

clean and cared for. They have the latest chopper bikes and Bay City Rollers gear. Susan is the black sheep of the family. It is almost as if the parents are ashamed of themselves because she is retarded and consequently take it out on her.

Her mother vents all her rage on Susan, and lets her go around dirty and neglected, begging strangers in the street for money. A man interfered with her once when she was out after dark. This had a traumatic effect on Susan and she lost her speech completely for a week. They never caught the man and you would have thought the mother would have learnt a lesson, but not one bit of it.

Susan still goes into all the little shops, getting free chips and the odd ten-pence piece. Her appearance is so pathetic that she shames everyone into giving her things.

Today she asks me for money and I tell her I do not have any. What she is really asking me for is love.

'Thank you for the picture, Susan,' and I pin it up.

She is always curious to see if I have acquired anything new in the way of possessions. Today her eyes are attracted to a bar of expensive soap which is lying on the table.

'What's that?'

'My favourite soap.'

'Can I sniff it?'

'If you like.'

She picks up the bar in its red and gold wrapping paper and holds it to her nose, half shutting her eyes in ecstasy. My existence is fairly frugal in many ways but I must have a few little luxuries. I always pay a pound for my deodorant stick, buy smoked salmon in Ridley Row market, and have a weakness for asparagus and broccoli spears. Life is very humdrum on a constant diet of baked beans and baths in Lifebuoy.

'Ooh! Lovely!'

I watched Susan sadly. What was it like to be her? To be surrounded by ugliness, by harsh, strident voices, muddy colours and rough textures. Never to meet an improving influence because she was so unattractive. How many opportunities do you get to encounter a Professor Higgins shelf-filling at Sainsburys or machining in Leather Lane?

'Can I 'ave it?'

'I would give it to you, but all the shops are closed, so I couldn't get any more for myself.'

'Please buy me some,' she pleads, with the dull turquoise eyes.

'O.K. On pay day.' And I promptly forgot all about it.

Susan never forgets. On the Thursday she lopes towards me in her too-long skirt and too-small shoes. 'Where's me soap?' she demands, and I feel ashamed because she has reminded me of my vague promise, so I give her the money and pat her head and say: 'Don't let anyone else in the family use it. It's Susan's soap 'cos it's special and,' I added defiantly, 'they can stop calling you Smelly.'

In the middle of a game of cards surrounded by Debbie, Tom, Martin and David. We sit with the two wooden benches turned towards one another in the shadow-streaked eight o'clock park.

Enter Susan's mother. 'We don't want yer fucking charity,' she says, and chucks a small parcel in my lap. A knife has ripped off half the paper and made slash marks in the soap—a stab in Susan's heart.

Muggers

October. The other evening at six o'clock I was walking along Upper Street crying my eyes out. I was badly shaken, and cold, and what I needed more than anything else was a drink. I went into the Wine Bar and ordered a large port and lemon. Fortunately the place was practically empty and the kindly chap behind the bar gave me a slightly quizzical glance with his 'nice to see you', but realised I wanted to be alone.

Tactfully he indicated an empty seat by the fireplace and remarked thoughtfully, 'You look as though you need warming up.'

My hands were shaking so much that I slopped some of the drink as I raised the glass. God, I thought, I really do feel like quitting the parks after this.

A few moments later a kindly middle-aged man I know walked in and came and sat opposite me.

'Hello, there. How are you?'

'All right, thanks.' I did not feel like crying on anyone's shoulder just yet. I was still suffering from shock.

We made small talk for a while about his job, a row the night before with his wife, the weather, and then, as we often did, decided to have a bash at the *Guardian* crossword. I have only very recently become something of a crossword addict. I can complete the prize-winner in the *Sunday People* but only seem to be able to get about three clues in the *Guardian* on my own. However, the mental stimulation of a hardened veteran works wonders. Tom was able to trigger off my rather limited logicality. Tonight I was really trying exceptionally hard because I wanted to take my mind off the experience of half an hour ago. However, Tom is a very perceptive man.

'I'm sure that word is "ensconced".'

'You're almost certainly right.'

'There are two c's, aren't there?' The pen felt clumsy between my fingers.

'Your hands are shaking.'

I try to appear unconcerned. 'Are they?'

'Maybe you need a spell on the wagon, or is there something else?'

'Please get me another large port and one for yourself.' I proffered a pound note but he waved it away and walked away to return with our drinks.

'What happened?'

I took a king-size gulp.

'I've been kind of attacked on the park.'

'What do you mean "kind of"?'

'I was sitting in the hut writing a letter. Round about half past five. It was dark and I was almost due to close. A black youth I had never seen before stuck his head round the door and asked if I had any matchboxes. I asked him if he collected them, but was rather surprised as I had never seen him before and wondered how he knew I was a matchbox addict. He pointed to two boxes on the table and asked if he could have them. I told him "Yes" and went to pick them up, whereupon he kicked the door open and dived in, followed by about five others.'

'How old were they?'

'Twelve to fifteen, but big—mostly taller than me. They were all over the hut, picking things up and trying to snatch the bag I was holding. I scuffled with them and two fell half on top of me. It was all a bit of a performance but after we had wrestled about a bit I managed to get outside, leaving a couple of them in the hut. The others were still trying to grab my bag and I ran round to the garage and came back with two hefty blokes.'

'Did they nick anything?'

'A little boy's football.'

'It sounds a very disturbing experience, but you're so shaken up . . . is there something else?'

'Well, it certainly made my bottle twitch—attempted robbery and the way they came bursting in. One of them could have had a knife. The leader kept one hand in his pocket all the time.'

'Your glass is empty.'

What I could not really explain to Tom, and what disturbed me most of all, was the way they touched me when we were struggling in that hut. They touched me with a frightening intimacy. The fact that the youths were blacks and half-castes made me feel even more reluctant to go to the police; there is so much anti-black feeling in this area. After all, we are not very far from Hoxton where the National Front has a fairly strong following. I recently had an article published in *West Indian World*, a non-political article, simply detailing my own personal experiences, in the main good experiences, with black people. As I gulped my fourth large port I reflected that they had certainly picked on the wrong person. But they had looked at me with real hatred, and the way they had run their hands over me while I was trying to escape had been a deliberate attempt to degrade me. Not for myself alone, but for what I stood for, white and in authority, though God knows I have always tried to play my authority down. Ridiculous to be a dictator over a small patch of concrete! One of the reasons that I got on so well with the kids was the fact that I was trying to get away from the old park-keeper image, the crusty uniformed figure with the officious bark of a serviceman or prison wardress. Now this had to happen!

Tom did persuade me to go to the police but it took a hell of a lot of persuasion. For a kick-off I hate going into cop shops. I am sure that the majority of our policemen are wonderful, but I always feel guilty and uncomfortable in a police station. This probably stems from the time when I went to stand bail for someone—which they later jumped—and was kept waiting in a tiny windowless room for over an hour. I identified myself too strongly with former occupants of that room.

I played down the situation when I was talking to the police. No, I did not wish to press charges or take the matter further—i.e., identifying them. I merely said they told me they had come from the Packington Estate which was notorious for knife-fights, muggings and gang warfare. However, it was a rather large estate and they could easily have told me that they came from there out of bravado, attempting to appear tough. Would they please just be kind enough to send a squad-car around about closing time, or let the Old Bill stroll by my park as part of his beat? They assured me that they would do this.

There have been rather a lot of muggings recently around the New North Road/Essex Road area. It is a rather depressed area. Newly-built (and in the main jerry-built) estates (not high-rise, only four storeys) have sprouted up everywhere. The present park is situated on a building site where more new flats are being constructed as part of the slum-clearance development. Our park is not far from Popham Street which before the coming of the council flats was a real dump. 'Cathy Come Home' and 'Poor Cow' used the old tenement buildings for certain sequences.

Much of the mugging has taken place outside or near the Essex Road Bingo Hall. As Christmas approaches the muggings will no doubt increase. It is advisable if you have a win at Bingo to call a taxi and stay on to the bitter end.

I saw a very well-made film recently. 'Death Wish', the vigilante brilliantly portrayed by Charles Bronson. It was about mugging in New York and there were some very strong scenes. The film was supposed to serve as a deterrent and I was very impressed and saw it twice. However, one thing disturbed me. There was a very large proportion of black youths in the audience. The majority of the muggers in the film were black.

Recently the National Front staged a demonstration in the East End. Their campaign was supposed to be about anti-mugging, but it had definite racist overtones. There has also been a great deal of adverse publicity given to the Brixton situation.

Were those young boys who burst in on me merely living up to an image inspired by press or television? Were they only acting as other people expected them to act? They did not really do me any harm, as I moved too fast and unexpectedly for them. But what are they going to turn into in two or three years time when they have built up an even deeper resentment because of the employment situation, the way they are depicted as behaving in films and newspapers, and the marches telling them to get back where they came from, when they were born in Islington and Hackney, have never set foot in Jamaica, and speak with cockney accents?

I have not seen any of those boys again. They must have been a wandering gang from the other side of the City Road or from the high, grey Barbican skyscrapers. Sometimes I hope I will see them again when they are not crazed with glue and hatred.

The incident left me feeling very sad and helpless.

Tina and Lee

There is so much around me that is wrong and yet so much that is beautiful in the simplicity of the things that ordinary people say. Their naïveté is rarely crude or vulgar.

Tina is seven. She looks up at me through a mist of brown hair, soft yellow-green eyes.

'I feel sorry for you, keep.'

'Why, Tina?' I am intrigued. 'Why should you feel sorry for me?'

She blushes, giggling, and her little earrings dance as she tosses her head from side to side.

'I can't tell you, keep.'

'Come on, Tina. I want to know,' I plead gently. Silvery peals of laughter.

''Cos you ain't got no tits,' and she runs away, long dark ringlets streaming, to the top of the slide, afraid of incurring my wrath. With a grin I shake my head pensively, squinting down at my thirty-two-inch T-shirt. Of course. She is thinking of her mother. A buxom Italian woman who is decidedly well-endowed. She pities me because I do not conform to her prototype. I am not what she expects.

Lee stands outside the door of the toilet, which is not working and which I always keep locked. He is four and wants to be Saint George today. Yesterday he was Batman. Tomorrow he will be a fireman. Lee is a child who loves me to fantasise with him.

'Why is that locked?'

'I have a baby dragon in there.'

'Really?' Cocking his ear against the door. 'I can't hear him snorting.'

'He's too young to snort yet. He can only really whistle through his nostrils. Not even as loud as a kettle.'

'I can't even hear that!'

'He's sleeping at the moment.'

'Can I see him?'

'Well, that's rather difficult.'

'Why?'

'He's a magic dragon. Well, all dragons are magic. He has very sensitive eyes.'

'What is sensitive?' (He never lets a new word pass him by.)

'Well, say you get a piece of dust in your eye, it makes you want to scratch. My dragon cannot see very well just yet. Like a new-born kitten. The light hurts his pupils so I can't let him out for exercise until the park closes.'

'Pupils? Like at school?'

'No. Pupils are these little black dots in your eyes.'

Holding out my hand-mirror to show him. 'See. You have them too.'

'Were they sensible when I was born?'

'Sensitive. Not sensible. Well, at first you could only pick out colours and shapes. Everything was a blur.'

'He's like that? Poorly dragon.'

'Oh, he'll soon grow.'

'Can I see him then?'

'He'll be too big for that toilet. He'll be too big for the park. See that giant crane over there?' I point towards the building site. 'He'll grow like that and breathe smoke and flames. I won't have room for him here. He'll be too fierce and too dangerous.'

'Don't worry, keep,' Lee says, complacently. 'I'll kill him for you.'

Oh, Lee will go far.

Punk

Last night I had a row with Brian about something very trivial. I threw a shoe at him and it smashed through the window, breaking a pane. I was rather disgusted with myself. Whatever is happening to me? Am I becoming submerged in the violence surrounding me? Is some of the aggro and anger rubbing off on me?

Youth is so dissatisfied. Paul has applied for a job with twenty other boys but his handwriting has let him down. I have tried laboriously to help him but words to him are a complete blind-spot. He has no sense of word or sentence construction and spells exactly as he talks, leaving all the 'h's off and sprinkling his prose with 'aints' and 'nothinks'.

We were talking about The Sex Pistols today. Pop-groups are an expression of the age we live in. The Dole Queue Babies might be a good name for a pop-group, we thought, and we started to write a song for them.

> *There ain't nothink much else for us to do*
> *But sit in the park just a sniffin' the glue.*
> *We're kind of tired of the ol' dole queue*
> *'Cos we're the Dole Queue Babies ...*

'That's great,' said Martin.
'It's just an echo of the times.'
'Yeah, but you understand.'
'Sort of,' I said, meditatively scratching the scar where a piece of flying glass had embedded itself in my wrist.

Gary also called in to see me today after a disastrous interview for a job in a warehouse.
'This poof says to me, "You got a high standard of literacy, young man?" "I most certainly have," I tell him, feeling right cocky. Job is a right dawdle. "Tell me, are you self-motivated?" "No. Sorry, guv. Don't drive," I tells him. "Next please," he yells. Can't understand what went wrong. What's up, keep? What you falling about like that for? It's not bleedin' funny.'
When I have recovered I say: 'Don't worry. There's other jobs.'
'I know, but I'm pissed off.'
'Well, don't go on the Evo.'
'No. I'm going down the Pack for a pint.'
'Enjoy that,' and I turn away on the pretext of putting the kettle on.
Gary goes off muttering. 'Funny? What's so bleedin' funny? Even keep is taking the piss out of me.'

Talking to Martin

Today he is sixteen. Wordlessly, I hand him a birthday card on which I have written: TO THE BEST HANDYMAN IN ISLINGTON. He laughs at this but I am remembering the times when he mended my fire, fixed the light switches and brought me the carpet-sweeper. The times when he was not being bloody-minded but constructive.

'I bought you a little something.'

Slightly embarrassed, I give him the model kit for a battleship. I hoped he wouldn't think I was regarding him as a child and so, with some misgivings, I had added twenty fags. He appeared surprisingly thrilled with the model and we went out together to buy some glue, as the shop will only serve minors with letters from parents. The assistant gave me an odd look. Maybe he thought I was a corrupter of juveniles.

We went back to the park and he sat quite happily building his boat. I sat beside him, completely absorbed, so that the bag of chips between us grew cold and greasy and had to be thrown to the pigeons.

'I am not interested in girls but there's nothing wrong with me, is there?'

'It's perfectly normal.'

'Now take Tom. He's a good-looking kid, but I'm very ordinary. Wouldn't you say I had a very ordinary face? It's not the kind of face anyone would really notice in the street. People look at me and they don't really see me. It's like being the Invisible Man.'

'There is nothing wrong with your face. The features are even and regular. You aren't covered in spots or pimples. You're not fat. You've got a perfectly good face.'

This seems to reassure him and he carries on with his stubby little hands delicately inserting turrets and guns.

'Do you think I'll ever meet the right girl? Look at Tom. They're all drooling over him.'

'Tom likes the competition, but when you meet a girl I have a feeling it will be very serious and you'll probably be very much in love at the ancient age of twenty. Is that part of the hull too?'

'That is the base of the hull.'

'I see. It's quite neat really.' I keep slipping unconsciously into their idiom.

'If I had a wife I wouldn't let her go on the pill. I wouldn't want her to come to no harm. If she was taking a drug like that I'd worry all the time.'

I decided to change the subject.

'You're very good at mechanical things. I'm hopeless at anything to do with my hands. I was so grateful when you helped me with cleaning that time I went on holiday. Housework puts me into such a panic, especially when I have a guest coming. I was trying to wash the kitchen floor and the cats kept slithering around on the soap-suds and I got so fed up that I flung the rag and bucket down and burst into tears.'

He grinned and deftly added the British flag to one of the masts.

'You write nice stories anyhow.'

'Sometimes, but I'm not practical. You are clever in a way that I could never be. We're all put on the earth for different things. You can get an old radio out of a junk-yard and make it like new. Don't you see! You're going to fit into society. You're so practical and full of common sense. So I want no more of this complex about not being any use and being ugly. I think you're great. Why do you think I spend so much time in your company? I enjoy being with you.'

He smiled and looked up at me and I could tell he was pleased. Maybe he was sensitive enough to know that subconsciously I would like a son like him, and he so desperately needs love, ego-boosting and attention, that it hurts.

Then the spell of our friendship is broken. Rose comes in and announces that her husband has hit her with a coathanger. She pulls up a holey jumble-sale sweater, revealing great welts on her side.

'I'm takin' two of the kids to a 'ostel down Camden Town,' she announces, her jaw set defiantly like a pugnacious boxer's.

Martin lays the boat down gently and goes to make the tea.

I sit listening to the outpourings of woe. Sounds like six of one and half a dozen of the other.

One thing is for sure. The battleship will never be finished this evening.

Tom in the Restaurant

It must be the coldest day of the year. My hands are so stiff that I can hardly unlock the gate. It is a Sunday morning. I put the fire and the kettle on immediately, blowing on my fingers trying to keep warm.

I am surprised to see Tom.

'You need a big coat in this weather.'

'I thought you'd get no visitors today and would be lonely.'

'That was nice of you. Good thing I don't work on commission.'

There is a strained look in his blue eyes staring at me from the cherubic face. He seems worried and perplexed and is fiddling with the doorlock in a preoccupied way.

Tom is hiding something from me. Has he pulled another job?

We play cards all morning over the half-door of the hut.

Every so often I ask him if he is cold, and shouldn't he be going home? But he seems to want to be near me. I am tempted to ask him into the hut, only the foreman has not been and it would put me in a compromising position if he found a fifteen-year-old boy sitting beside me.

He plays rummy badly as though his mind is on other things. I try to draw him out but there is a barrier and I know he wants to confide but is too afraid or ashamed to tell me.

By twelve o'clock I am starving and I decide to walk down to Upper Street to the rather chic restaurant where they specialise in American-style beefburgers.

'What time is your dinner?'

'About half one.'

'Well, providing you don't mind watching me eat you can come too.'

He looks pleased at the prospect. I promise him a cup of coffee.

He feels awkward and ill at ease in the restaurant. We sit down at the polished brown table with its Scandinavian cutlery and when the two menus are put in front of us Tom pulls out a Mars bar, rips off the wrapping and starts to demolish it.

People stare at us curiously. The restaurant is full of expensively dressed Islington trendies. Leather coats and sleek long hair, Elton John glasses and woolly ski-helmets.

I order a king-size steakburger for myself, medium rare, with salad, and a glass of red wine, with a coffee for Tom.

'Why ain't there a cloth on this table? You'd think they'd be able to afford one in a place like this,' he says loudly.

I ignore the remark and indicate some newspapers that have been left out for the customers. He triumphantly returns with the *News of the World* which he starts to devour avidly.

His coffee arrives complete with a small copper jug of milk and the salad for my meal.

'There ain't arf a lot of milk in this jug for the one cup. Can I drink it all?'

The couple on the next table raise their eyebrows expressively at one another. They are talking loudly and arrogantly about a Pasolini film on at Islington Green. At least Tom is being himself.

At last my meal and a glass of wine arrive.

'Can I 'ave a chip?'

'Help yourself.'

More eyebrows raised. He shows an interest in my wine, and thinking what-the-hell, I invite him to take a sip. He pulls a very wry face and splutters. ''Ow ever can you drink that? It ain't arf sour.'

'It's a taste you get used to. When you are young you like sweet things but as you get older your taste-buds mellow and you start craving for bitter flavours.'

He takes a bar of Cadbury's Flake out of his pocket and starts to tackle that. Pieces of chocolate are falling all over the newspaper.

'Tom,' I plead. 'Do you have to show me up?'

People are looking at him with compassion and at me with anger. Whatever does it look like? A mother liberally guzzling an enormous Sunday dinner watched by a starving son who has to make do with chocolate bars?

I am more than relieved when they bring the bill and as soon as it arrives begin to put my coat on.

Tom puts a hand in the pocket of his bomber jacket and pulls out a wad of notes.

''Ere, you're always treating me. Let me pay.'

'Of course not. It's far too much. Nearly three pounds,' I snap.

'I'd like to.'

'No. Come on. For Christ's sake put that money away,' I mutter under my breath.

Outside in the late November street he is silent again and moody and slouching.

I glance at him sideways but he continues staring straight ahead.

'Wherever did you get all that money from?'

'It's not mine.'

'Well, that's pretty obvious. Where is it from?'

'I'm looking after it for someone,' he says vaguely, beginning to whistle tunelessly through the gap in his otherwise perfect front teeth.

It is no use trying to probe any further. He has shut up like a clam, and although I know he likes and values my friendship he does not feel he can tell me everything about himself. Maybe he just likes to appear enigmatic.

Then he shows another side to his personality.

'Sorry about what I was like back there only I've never been in a place like that before. I couldn't stand the people. All pretending to be something they're not. Looking at me like I was off another planet. I just thought I bet I got more in my pocket than you lot all put together.'

It was one of the longest speeches he had ever made. I began to feel for his awkward class-consciousness. I identified more with him than with the Canonbury diners.

'Didn't care for them much meself.'

He grins and says almost affectionately: 'Well, you're one of us.'

'I'm glad.'

'We're even learning you to speak proper.'

'Yeah. You are, mate.'

We walk back into the deserted park and Tom behaves like a little boy again, chasing the seagulls with flapping arms.

Sunday Dinner

Sunday again. I am relieving on a tiny park this week with a hut like a telephone kiosk and no room to cook. Looking for somewhere to eat, I prowl up and down New North Road and Essex Road cursing, my tummy rumbling uncontrollably.

Eventually I find a café and I go inside to be greeted by that damp, dirty smell. Unwashed bodies and old raincoats. It is full of single, shabby, middle-aged blokes mainly on their own. A sad sight. Refugees from bed-sitters and bed-and-breakfast houses. A pretty lonely life, and what a place to come and eat your Sunday dinner in!

I sit, elbows on table, hungry but nervous about eating, unable to overcome a certain squeamishness that I have always had about some cafés not being clean. It is not always the people who run them but the denizens who create the problem. Invariably, when I am about to tuck into my plate of bacon and eggs some old dosser will come and sit opposite me. He will start picking his nose or spitting on the butt of his home-made fag or talking to me with his mouth full. I have tremendous compassion for my fellow men, except when I am eating.

The waitress is Greek, cross-eyed and short-tempered. 'What you want?'

'Lamb chop. And would you mind telling me what the two vegetables are?'

'Chips and peas,' she raps.

'Could I possibly have mash? It's O.K. about the peas.'

'You'll have to wait.'

'That's all right. Happy New Year.'

She scowls at me and strides away.

Half an hour later, when the meal arrives, it appears to be submerged in what can only be described as dirty washing-up water. I try a few mouthfuls, nearly gagging on them, and hastily beat a retreat. The sight of the cook passing my plate through the hatch with a fag in her mouth did not help.

By complete contrast, I enter a very elegant Canonbury pub full of people talking through their noses about social work, problems with their gardens and the aggravation of sitting tenants in their properties. Everyone seems to be wearing expensive woolly cardigans and smoking pipes.

I order a Guinness and ask if there is anything to eat. They do not even sell crisps. Languidly, the landlady points to plates of cubed cheese, pickled onions and wafer biscuits. I must look as though I come from the wrong end of the Essex Road for she says primly: 'They are on the house,' with a knife-edge to her voice.

All the other people are probably so well fed and so absorbed in their own ego-trips that they are giving no attention to the plates.

I do a shameful thing. I start to wolf down the lot. The landlady is giving me some very strange looks from under her Thatcher-like mass of hair. I order another Guinness to try to account for my presence. It is no good. I cannot stop eating until the plates are empty. I do not feel I am being selfish, as there are other dishes scattered around the bar. I have to force back the desire to move around and start attacking them.

I cannot get out of that pretentious bar fast enough. People are looking at me with a mixture of compassion and disgust. God, is that the expression I put on when a dosser sits opposite me?!

Back in the park the kids known by the other children as 'Squatters' are waiting for me.

'Where you been, keep?'

I like these funny, scruffy little children because they are so affectionate and always run up for a cuddle. They are also very polite and never ask me for money. When I first came they used to play me up a lot so that I told them they would have to leave. The five of them stood like a little wall opposite me, singing 'We shall not be moved'. They must have learnt this from their parents.

The house where they are squatting is really dilapidated with no curtains at the windows and naked bulbs hanging from the ceilings.

The kids told me they came from Jamaica and wanted to go back there.

I unlocked my hut door. The five of them stood and peered in.

'You had your dinner, keep?'

'Not really. I'm supposed to cook in this!'

'What a ras place!'

'Keep, you must be hungry.'

'No, I'm all right.'

Their concern touches me and I give them each a couple of sugar lumps as I do not have any sweets. They champ away like five small brown colts. They chatter away vivaciously and I put some reggae on the little transistor and we start dancing about to keep warm. We are so preoccupied that I do not notice that the eldest girl has slipped quietly off.

Some time later she returns, carrying a tray with a plate covering another plate to keep it warm.

'We had too much food, keep, so I brought some for you.'

I feel choked by their kindness, and when I uncover the dish I see that it is composed mainly of rice and peppers and yams.

'Here's some tabasco, keep. I didn't put it on 'cos it's very hot. You got to take it easy, man.'

I looked down at the plate and then up at the five grinning faces.

'I'm really going to enjoy this. It's the first time I've had a West Indian Sunday dinner.'

I could not thank them enough and sat contentedly eating and watching them dance in the deserted winter park.

Can You Hear Me?

I have been given a plant for the hut. I do not know what it is called but it has large red berries like small tomatoes. The children say it is a Christmas plant and only comes out in late November. How can they know when they have no gardens?

The plant is sad and drooping and looks as though it is dying. I feel for it. The smaller greenish berries look as though they will never ripen because they are wrinkled, so I am gentle with the plant. It has been starved of nourishment so I do not want to give it too much of a shock, and fill half a cup of water. I sprinkle it carefully with my hand three times a day. At least it will not die of frostbite.

In my hut there is a single-bar electric fire high up near the roof and this beams down on the plant. I hope it thinks it is the benevolent winter sun.

Last night at the hospital I was feeding a man who had had a stroke. He was paralysed all down the right side and as I fed him he kept jerking his head about. His eyes were very conscious of everything around him and I thought he would like me to talk even though he could not answer. Can he hear me?

'It was very cold on the park today and the gulls came down. They're much greedier than the pigeons and very swift. They dive in and grab all the crumbs. There's a good boy. I'm glad you're eating all your food.'

His left hand groped for mine and I found he was holding my fingers tightly in the way that the gypsy cat clasps me with her claws. I squeezed his hand back hard. He was making such an effort to finish the mashed-up baby food, and I kept on talking about the birds and the children and the tricks they got up to. I felt he could understand me.

After I had finished feeding him he lifted my hand to his lips and kissed it. Then he gestured to a bowl of sweets on the side of the locker. I smiled and took one, wiped his face clean, picked up the old, worn yellowed hand and pressed it against my face. Then I had to get out into the kitchen and help with the washing-up, because I can only act tough on the ward for so long.

Soon I was laughing and joking with the orderly from Madrid in my very rusty schoolgirl Spanish.

'George is playing up tonight,' I told her. 'Chucked all his bed clothes off. Threw a bowl of soup on the floor.'

'Bloody hell,' she said. '*Madre de dios! No entiendo los viejos.*'

'They're like children and they only want love.'

In the pub that night drinking with the porters, swapping stories, anecdotes about patients, some funny, some sad.

The wealthy OAP stands me a Guinness. She is a cunning old devil and always does this, and when I have to return the compliment says: 'Oh how nice of you, dear, but I've really had too much heavy stuff. I'll have a large scotch, thank you.'

Tonight she rather irritates me and I tell her: 'You shouldn't have done that. I'm on a budget at the moment and I don't like getting involved.'

She pretends to be deaf when it suits her as well.

'A budgie. You got a budgie? My neighbour's got one of them. Nice little birds.'

'A budget, not a budgie!' I almost shouted.

'I can't hear you!' she yelled back belligerently and joyfully.

The next morning I opened the hut and saw a great transformation in the plant. The leaves were standing up straight. No more berries had fallen into the pot and it looked as though it was smiling at me with the red glossy fruit. I read somewhere that you should talk to flowers. 'You look better today,' I said, as I sprinkled a few more drops of water around the earth at its roots.

I felt that it could hear me and that it understood.

Will They Make It?

On the ward as I look around me I notice that there are some men who are going to make it and others who are bound to go under. Some people have the will to live, like the charming man of sixty surviving his fourth coronary, still ebullient and cheerful. 'I love people. That's all that matters to me. I like my little shop and getting to know my customers and watching their children growing up. I have a small tailoring business in Stoke Newington. I take my wife out to the theatre once a week and to dinner. Being back here is an awful bind but it won't be for long.' I am convinced that he will pull through yet again.

Another man I regularly visit is about the same age but rapidly slipping into a senile decline. 'I won't get out of here alive. That's for sure. On the other hand they might stick me into an old people's home to finish me off. They say I don't need this stick to get about with, but I do—I do. I need them to help me wash and dress; it's the nurse's fault that I broke two ribs. Nobody cares. When I'm in an old people's home they'll be glad I'm there to be finished off.'

Geriatric ramblings are never very pleasant to listen to because they are invariably full of self-pity. Yet according to the medical experts this man need not be geriatric. He has just given up caring and lost that fierce independence which characterises so many old people. He has given up on survival.

I draw a parallel between the playground and the hospital because getting close to the adolescents I cannot help speculating about their future. There are those who will make it and others who cannot help but fall by the wayside.

Paul will make it, I feel sure. The glue craze is only a phase he is going through. Losing his father so suddenly has left him with a feeling of great insecurity. He found he could lead the sniffers but he will grow out of that. Working on the building site and looking twenty instead of sixteen has made him mature rather too early in certain directions. Yet it is good that he is in the company of older men. He is beginning to find pleasure in a pint of beer, a game of cards and the easy camaraderie you get from workmates. He will end up as a foreman or a ganger and probably learn some skilled trade.

I deliberately cut out the story of the boy who died from sniffing glue. It was on the front page of the *Islington Gazette*. I stuck it up on the wall of my hut and it looked incongruous in the middle of my little art gallery among drawings of Mickey Mouse, Jaws, Bambi and prehistoric animals. In an attempt to brighten up the grim walls I had invited the children to bring me their own paintings and sketches and the response was tremendous. At least the inside of the hut looked cheerful and inviting. I could do little about the outside with its flaking paint of utilitarian green. As the premises were only temporary the council did not want me to paint the hut. In a way it had a kind of seedy Victorian charm even though someone had nicked the decorative ball from the roof. The pointed top made me think of deserted piers at the end of the season and the *fin de siècle* atmosphere in rainy bus shelters on lonely promenades. The outside of my hut belonged to the council but the inside was my own and the children's, and it was amazing that there were so many talented young artists around.

Paul stood looking in.

'See that?' I asked him grimly, pointing at the newspaper cutting. 'Could have been one of your followers. One of your admirers.'

Paul looked ashamed and fidgeted with his identity bracelets and gazed everywhere but at me.

'Don't do it no more, keep. Don't take Evo no more.'

'Glad to hear it. If you were my son I wouldn't mind you drinking beer, though. You're big enough and ugly enough, as my old gran used to say.'

'You ain't old enough to be my mum.'

'Don't you be so sure.' But I blushed and felt pleased inside.

Debbie will make it. Now she is fourteen I have managed to get her a job in a hairdressers on Saturdays. She is pretty and competent, full of life and energy. That day we spent in Hampstead had been most enjoyable because of her simple vivacity. She is not academically bright, not interested in books or classical music, but she is very sharp. I like the way she draws. She has a flair for dressing simply but tastefully and at times looks quite stunning. She could become a model. She is doing well at hairdressing; maybe she will have her own shop one day. I have noticed her skill at card games, the quickness of her mind when we are playing Monopoly. Yes, I can see her as a business woman.

Tom, I am frankly not sure about. He has got in with a bad lot and been in trouble for breaking and entering.

Nothing very serious, but it has gone against him and now, after being cautioned, he has a record. Next time it will be at best probation, at worst six months' detention. I hope there is no next time but, unfortunately, it is a question of the company he keeps. Another bad factor is the admiration and adoration he has for his elder brother who is constantly in trouble. He is obviously trying to imitate him and sees him more as a father-figure than his own father. Tom regards his father with contempt: 'You should have seen me old man the other night. He was staggering along the road talking to the lamp-posts and when they wouldn't answer him he got mad and started talking to the traffic meters.'

When he talks about his brother and the jobs he has pulled—'They never did find them sawn-off shotguns. H. is too clever'—his eyes light up. When he heard I had been in the Isle of Wight he said: 'Me bruvver was there. In the nick. That's why you never got to meet him.' I have tried to reason with him that petty thieving is just not worth it and if H. is so clever how come he is always doing time? Tom does not want to lose the heroic image, the conception he has of his brother as a second Biggs, the Al Capone of the City Road.

The influences around Tom are a great pity. He is a bright lad, quick-thinking and quick-talking. I was surprised how rapidly he learnt to play chess. He has a really beautiful face of extraordinary innocence. A baby's face with candid blue eyes superimposed on a slim angular body—he is about five foot eight, which is tall for fifteen. He walks awkwardly because his limbs are so long, and he flaps his hands about a great deal when he is talking—a mannerism which could be interpreted as effeminacy. In reality, though, he simply feels all legs, arms and fingers.

His school work is suffering because of his obsession with crime and criminology. Sometimes he will sit for hours on the park bench, simply doing nothing, yet completely at ease. I have never seen a boy so ready to relax. He can gaze into space for two hours at a time, his legs sprawled out nonchalantly in front of him, the long ungainly arms resting along the back of the seat.

'What are you thinking about, Tom?'

'Nothink.'

'How can you sit like that? Don't you get bored? We could play chess or cards if you like.'

Tom moves slightly, lowering his head on to his shoulder and closing his eyes with the thick brown lashes.

'I'm conserving my energy,' he mumbles.

I am surprised to hear him use a word like 'conserving', and ask him to explain what he means.

'Well, if I rest a lot now I shall have bags of energy for when I'm older. Then I can commit the perfect crime because I won't have used up all my reserves while I'm young.'

This sounded so logical and he had expressed himself so well that I looked at him with a new respect.

Maybe I get on so well with children because I have not really grown up myself. I tend to fantasise like Walter Mitty. One of my dreams is of becoming a successful market trader, and I am trying to save up for a stall. I have asked Tom to help me run one and he has agreed. I have a feeling he would do very well in a market with his blarney and pretty face. I wish I had two hundred pounds to take him in hand and to get myself established. God knows he needs someone to divert him from the world of petty thieves, small-time cons and the high-rise slabs of concrete that are supposed to be homes.

In Kestrel House, City Road, a young mother threw herself out of the window the other night from the fourteenth floor. The report said that she had been drinking and had had a row with her husband. Maybe she had just given up and realised she was never going to make it. I'd hate that to happen to any of my children.

Spring

Sometimes I think I shall leave the park. Not doing anything active, because it is the winter and no children come to play, I am reminded of the Gentle Giant in Oscar Wilde's children's story, standing in his big castle looking over the snow-covered deserted garden. If only one little boy would come in and sit on a swing and smile and bring some life into the frost-sprinkled patch of concrete.

But today, today is different. It is the third of March and the sun has bravely started to shine and I walk through the other parks on the way to collect my wages. Mauve and yellow crocuses delicately poking their shell-like ears from the white-green grass. John, the Polish gardener in Canonbury, says: 'Bloody birds. Always attacking the yellow. It's the colour.' John scowls from beneath his black beret. 'They don't touch the purple ones.'

'Birds are attracted to yellow and gold. Maybe that's why the pigeon shat on my hair the other day.'

He grins, and his face splits into myriads of furrows. A face that has been around for a long while and been dwelt in. 'Never mind. Gentlemen prefer blondes.'

Encouraging to see old people sitting well wrapped up in chunky coats, holding their knobbed sticks, on the benches along New River Walk.

'Will the ducks be here soon?' I ask Joe.

'Any time now. How are yer, me darlin'?' Irish Joe, tall and white haired, with the figure of a boy and twinkling blue eyes which mock me.

''Tis grand to see the old people out and about again.' He points to the benches. Conversations are going on about pensions, meals-on-wheels, home-helps and the squatting scandal.

'I was going to leave the parks.'
'You never were.'
'The winter got me down this year.'
'But not now?'
'Not now, Joe. The blossom will soon be out on your trees.'
'I was thinking that meself.'
'What an exquisite day!'

Joe hands me a large blue-and-white striped mug full of strong sweet tea, almost black. Although I do not take sugar it tastes good. But then I am in love with the spring, coming to take the parks by surprise, bringing the soft green smells and the pink and white headdresses for the trees, the ducks and their ducklings, the daffodils and the sounds of laughter and the children sliding and see-sawing and shrieking in imaginary terror. But some things will never return.

They do not seem to play any more. When did I last see a game of marbles? Someone blowing bubbles? A home-made wooden scooter? A Punch and Judy show? Jumping beans which you could buy outside the cinema on Saturday morning? The man coming up from the floor in the plush old cinema in a haze of bright pink flourescence to play the organ while we sang 'I've got a lovely bunch of coconuts.' Sitting in the back row with Danny, both of us aged eight, clasping hands sticky from Spangles, vowing our undying love for one another. Was it all so very long ago?

Today is the fast, flash age. The chopper bikes purr swiftly by, the frozen peas boiling welcome them home, the school tells them how babies are born and shows them films before they have learnt how to tell the time, they sit glued to the television screen, and no one bothers to make a scooter out of old bits of wood. What is the point in making anything? The new affluence, while it lasts, can buy nearly everything.

Jubilee!

The streets look so pretty today—Jubilee Sunday—as I sit in my park watching the lines of small flags fluttering from the little houses and the council blocks. Debbie and Tom come to meet me, and as there is no one in the park we decide to walk and see what is going on everywhere.

Debbie is wearing a red, white and blue sun dress and looking absolutely stunning. Small union jack earrings swing from her brown shell-like ears. Tom, who is decidedly unpatriotic, stumps along beside us in his usual denim gear, muttering that it is all a 'load of cobblers' and that the Punks have got the right idea. They have evidently designed a T-shirt which portrays Her Majesty with a safety-pin stuck through her nose and the words: 'God save the queen 'cos she ain't no human being'. I am not amused and I think very few people are, and find the idea sad rather than shocking.

It is curious. I was never conscious of having royalist feelings before but I am caught up in the emotional colour around me. We pass into a street full of ghastly tenement houses which should have been demolished years ago and the flags trailing across the crumbling stucco fronts hurt my eyes with their brightness. It is easily the biggest and best display yet and I notice that there is a street party going on and all the children look immaculate and all seem to be wearing new clothes. Susan runs to me with red bows in her blonde hair and clad in a dazzling white dress like a commercial for soap powder.

'Aren't I a nice clean girl today?' She twirls around on one toe so that the frock flares out.

'You look smashing,' I tell her, and she gives me a pathetic grin which makes me feel choked.

Some of the mothers call me over to the tables. 'Wotcher, keep. 'Ave a bit of cake. 'Ave some lemonade.' They give me a paper hat which I put on, and it makes Tom guffaw. It has a big brim and shades my eyes from the sun. I pull a couple of crackers, trying not to win the big ends, and then it begins to rain and everyone curses and I start to help clear up the tables and carry crockery into doorways. An old girl is standing beside me and taps my arm. 'Remember the coronation, love?'

'Yes. I was ten.'

'Pretty as a picture, weren't she? I see it on the telly. She didn't 'arf look young, and wearing all them 'eavy ermines and that dirty great crown. I thought to myself, poor girl 'aving to go through all that and no toilet near by. They ought to 'ave public conveniences in Westminster Abbey.'

I smile at her and she wedges her finger into her mouth.

'Me dentures keep slippin',' she mutters apologetically. 'Too much rich food.'

'Do you remember VE day?' I ask her.

'Cor blimy yes, cock. But you wouldn't now, would you?'

'Well I was only three, but I seem to be able to. A bit, anyway. The scene was something like this but I don't think it rained.'

We stand watching the rain, which shows no sign of abating.

'They was good, them days. People was people in the war. They've lost something now.'

'I think a little of that feeling comes back at a time like this, don't you?'

She regards me steadily, shrewd black-button gypsy eyes. 'Maybe you're right, girl. Maybe it does.'

When the rain has ceased Debbie and Tom and I take a stroll along Essex Road. Debbie nudges me excitedly. A float is passing by composed entirely of children and depicting the Coronation scene. The little queen is chubby with fat black ringlets beneath her crown. With one hand she clasps the *papier mâché* sceptre and with the other dimpled palm waves disdainfully and regally at us. 'Loves 'erself, that one, but she does look pretty,' admits Debbie, grudgingly.

Tom has been paying no attention to the procession at all and is gazing with rapt fascination into the window of an antique shop at an exquisitely carved chess-table.

'Look at that, Gill,' he whispers in awe.

'I wonder how much they want for it,' I say longingly.

'I could lift it for you,' replies Tom predictably.

We go back to the park and as a special treat I make us coffee from the tiny jar costing seventy-five pence.

I have written a Jubilee poem for a *Sunday Mirror* competition and I read it to them. The judge is going to be Sir John Betjeman and I have unconsciously parodied his style with lines like:

> *White cricket figures upon the green*
> *Home-made jams and chintz curtains clean.*
> *Oh bring out the muffins for tea!*

It is all about the traditions and the freedom of England. They seem to like the poem, but at the lines:

> *But without our dear queen*
> *Sitting proud on the throne . . .*

Tom doubles up with laughter.

'You'll 'ave to change that, Gill.'

I frown at the words and think perhaps I should if it is going to have that kind of effect.

Walking Home

One of those beautiful balmy early June evenings. Brian comes to meet me just as I am locking up. 'G'night, keep,' shout the children as they troop off home in various directions.

We decide to walk home and savour the deliciously refreshing late Spring air and watch the sun going down around the chimney-pots.

Wandering along the Essex Road we pass a launderette and stand looking in. An elegant young woman wearing a pleated skirt, crisp white blouse, dark stockings and high-heeled shoes, appears to be in charge of the machines. She looks self-assured, competent and a trifle bossy. She turns towards us and her vibrant blue eyes break into a smile of recognition. I notice that she has plucked her eyebrows.

'That's never the pretty little kid you used to take up to the Heath last summer?'

'Yes. That's Debbie. Earning herself a bit of pocket money.'

'I would never have recognised her!'

'I know. They seem to grow up fast round here.'

I experienced a vague feeling of sadness. She waves at us and we wave back and continue on our way.

I start to talk to Brian about the kids.

I am helping Debbie with her French homework, went with her to choose her first brassière because she had felt self-conscious, and shown her how to use an interspacial toothbrush. (I have been having extensive dental treatment recently which has made me very aware of the importance of caring for children's teeth and I have been nagging the mums constantly to go and get their little ones' gums painted with fluoride.)

Martin has a chance to go into the printing trade, he told me today. I imagined it was a very closed shop but he proudly informed me that his grandfather had been on the Street all his life and was going to pull a few strings.

Tom confessed that he gave up 'nicking fings' over Lent and has decided to become a professional chess-player instead. To my annoyance and frustration he thoroughly wiped the board with me today. Not once, but *three times*, and considering I taught him everything I ought to be flattered but I'm not!

I heard that Gary was in hospital with a badly damaged lung caused by sniffing glue.

Rose has left the battered wives' home and gone back to her husband. She said: "E must think somefink of me or he wouldn't 'it me, would 'e? Give me two pounds for Bingo tonight.'

We cross Essex Road by the library and I suggest a stroll through New River Walk.

'But it's closed, luv.'

With a grin, I produce the duplicate council key from my pocket. Being a park-keeper has its advantages. Slowly, enjoying the fresh green smells, stooping to inspect the rockery plants, pausing by the willow tree, we wander on. I admire the way Polish John keeps his garden, the gentleness of his big stubby hands as he plants the delicate bulbs.

I remember how concerned he was about the great sweeping fronds of the weeping willow. They were keeping the sunlight away from his children. For some reason I thought of the Barbican towers looming and frowning ominously and shutting out hope and growth.

I lock Polish John's park and we cross the little road to Joe's gardens. 'I am sure he won't mind,' I say softly as I turn the key in the padlock. 'We might even catch the secret daffodil snatcher.'

'The who?'

I tell Brian about the hippy on Mothering Sunday,

standing outside the Duchess in a moth-eaten fur coat and floppy hat, selling daffodils at twenty pence a bunch. I admired his display and he winked and told me they had come off the council parks.

The ducks must be asleep for Joe's pond is deserted. We find a bench and sit contentedly in the gathering dusk. The traffic sounds are muffled and we can hear the birds singing themselves to sleep.

The last two years have matured me. Perhaps in a way going back to childhood helps to enhance and enrich one's sensibilities. I have had time to think and to question. To wonder and explore emotions. To see and feel deeply the agonies of adolescence all over again. It has been an exciting time, a kind of reincarnation. I have been able to drink in and absorb the opinions around me. I have been able to get to know a few people in depth. Those children have helped me to become myself through their own candour. Impossible to play false against such complete and sometimes brutal honesty! They will not need me much longer—Tom, Martin, Debbie and the others—but they will never realise how grateful I am to them.

I only hope I have done something for them too.